T0381945

NATURE MATTERS

NATURE MATTERS

Vital Poems from the Global Majority

EDITED BY

Mona Arshi &
Karen McCarthy Woolf

faber

First published in 2025
by Faber & Faber Ltd
The Bindery, 51 Hatton Garden
London, EC1N 8HN

Typeset by Typo•glyphix, Burton-on-Trent, DE14 3HN
Printed in the UK by Short Run Press

A CIP record for this book
is available from the British Library

ISBN 978–0–571–37028–3

Printed and bound in the UK on FSC® certified paper in line with our continuing
commitment to ethical business practices, sustainability and the environment.
For further information see faber.co.uk/environmental-policy

Our authorised representative in the EU for product safety is
Easy Access System Europe, Mustamäe tee 50, 10621 Tallinn, Estonia
gpsr.requests@easproject.com

2 4 6 8 10 9 7 5 3 1

CONTENTS

WATER

FIRE

INTRODUCTION

This anthology presents some of today's most urgent and inspirational poems engaging with the natural world and aligned by the principle that nature matters everywhere and for everyone and everything. It is also concerned with the question of whose voices we privilege and the themes to which our ears have become attuned. All anthologies, to some extent, hold such issues at heart. They exist to capture a particular moment of change or a more seismic shift in the landscape that amends and augments the archive. Intrinsically they attempt to redress an imbalance, or an injustice. Sometimes it takes the act of anthologising to know exactly what is missing, or to instigate necessary transformation. At least these are the guiding principles that shape *Nature Matters*, which invites us to reconsider the nature poem in this first quarter of the twenty-first century from global-majority perspectives.

Hardly a radical idea, although here in the UK it is novel. Twenty years ago, less than 1 per cent of published poets of colour had collections with mainstream presses. It has taken sustained activist interventions – via collectives, national mentoring schemes and publishing initiatives – to begin to amend the infrastructure and widen participation to create a more culturally diverse, and therefore accurate, picture. Now, poets of the global majority are part of a more inclusive space, although, when it comes to nature writing, what we might have to say *about* nature or how nature resides within the work has often been sublimated in favour of readings that focus on identity. In the United States, there have already been attempts to address this via broader discussions around race and the personal, while looking at the correlation between climate change and denial, alongside the dehumanising of migrants, and the tenacity and violence of racism. Camille

Dungy's anthology *Black Nature: Four Hundred Years of African American Nature Poetry* (University of Georgia Press, 2009) is explicit in its reckoning of how the history of African-American interaction with the land is shaped by whether a person is forced to vacate it or work on it, without wage, and with no right to dwell freely upon or to own it. As its title suggests, the edition both ventilates the voices and concerns that had been ignored and also problematises what a nature poem might do or be.

Perhaps the closest equivalent in the UK has been Jackie Kay, James Proctor and Gemma Robinson's anthology *Out of Bounds: British Black and Asian Poets* (Bloodaxe Books, 2012) – 'an alternative A to Z of the nation' – which expanded a poetry of place beyond a ghettoisation of the urban as locale to reach into rural, regional and suburban crevices. However, although that anthology was specific in its bid to represent poets of colour situated within and writing about a variety of environments, this does not by extension equal 'nature poetry'.

In *Nature Matters*, our definition of nature is all-encompassing so as to include everything within the planetary atmosphere along the deep geological timeline of the Anthropocene that is non-human and human (although not fabricated by humans or our machines). So, the sweep of shoreline along a turquoise coastline dotted with sand dollars, or migratory birds dipping their beaks for worms, or the leaves on London plane trees peeping out from rows of slate rooftops. And the wind. And steam from the chicken-shop chimney. And chickens, battery-farmed though they may be. And the teenagers in the queue, in their goose-down puffas, their breath pluming in the air. It is when we move from seeing nature as just an inevitable backdrop and consider its own agency and status that the possibilities of 'the nature poem' come into focus: something that has necessarily developed, expanded and been complicated from its pastoral origins and the Romantic gaze. There is greater awareness today of the potential for poetries of ecological protest and environmental witness. As Jason Allen-Paisant writes in these pages, 'It's time to write about daffodils / again'.

It was against this backdrop in 2020 that Mona Arshi, as poet-in-residence and novice birdwatcher at Cley Marshes in Norfolk, wrote a tweet asking, 'Where are our Black and Asian nature writers?' The response was prolific. The poets were there; so, too, the poems. While some more recent nature poetry anthologies have diversified to include more poets of colour, until now there has been no single volume dedicated to the exploration of nature poetry by Black, Asian and global-majority poets in the UK. None that give space to consider how our relationships with nature play out – as migrants, as children and grandchildren and great-grandchildren of migrants, as newly settled and native citizens in a place that we too share and shape. If England's green spaces have historically been seen as hostile to certain communities, how do their encounters differ? How does culture intersect with poem-making? These same questions and sense of exclusion, particularly in the light of climate catastrophe and mass species extinctions, had also prompted Karen McCarthy Woolf to take action and pursue doctoral research exploring ways in which poetry might challenge a Eurocentric bias in ecopoetics. Together, as poets of colour whose work was deeply enmeshed in the creative thrall of the 'more-than-human', our mutual experiences chimed.

And so *Nature Matters* came into being as a venture which seeks to spotlight a comprehensive range of poetry from the past fifty years that brings new or overlooked insight and experience to the question of what qualifies as nature poetry and who is writing it. The poets gathered here, all of whom have published at least one collection, grapple with this terrain using myriad approaches that loop across generations and anglophone nations. The anthology's contours trace a twentieth-century, post-war and subsequent postcolonial era, when the edifice of the British Empire began to shift and disintegrate, and migrant communities from the Caribbean, Africa and Asia became more ubiquitous and firmly established. The vast majority of those who came to the UK settled in cities, and access to the countryside and coastal towns was rarer – as poems such as Roger Robinson's 'The City Kids See the Sea' and Raymond Antrobus's 'City Boy Talks to Trees' suggest. With these factors in mind, the anthology limits its representation of US poets to those published in the UK with roots in Africa, the Caribbean, India and the British constellation as described. The selection is not exhaustive, but it showcases a vibrant range of voices and formal approaches. Many poems are totally new, written specially for the anthology and offering insight into today's most pressing preoccupations. To give a sense of antecedent, key foundational poems have been selected such as 'Small Questions Asked by the Fat Black Woman' by Grace Nichols, E. A. Markham's 'The Sea' and Kamau Brathwaite's 'Loss of the Innocents' from *Strange Fruit* (Peepal Tree Press, 2016), which is emblematic to this anthology's spirit of resilience, movement and fluidity. We find poems that feature insects, snails, fruit, fauna and weather as well as lakes and volcanoes, the domestic world of the garden and, of course, trees. There are poems that remind us of ancient Indigenous wisdom and cultural histories obliterated by colonisation, such as those expressed in Karthika Naïr's 'Women of Uttarakhand, I did not know your names', which offers an account of the women of the Chipko movement who, centuries ago, saved a holy tree from extinction.

The anthology is divided into four sections: 'Earth', 'Air', 'Water' and 'Fire'. In 'Earth', Kei Miller's 'Unsettled' takes the reader deep inside Jamaican 'country' and back to a precolonial era via the 'unflattened and unsugared fields' to a 'tegareg / sprawl of roots and canopies'. It is a sonorous paean to the thicket, to unapologetic wildness, that encourages a decolonised reading of the landscape beyond the European institutions that shaped it. This decoloniality is echoed in Malika Booker's 'Songs of Mahogany' where the architectural and interior vernacular of the 'big house' is repositioned in the light of plantocracy, as a genocide where 'men laboured in the art of such a thing'. We sink into earth in Ishion Hutchinson's incantatory excerpt from *School of Instructions*, a book-length poem that recreates the horror of the trenches for West Indian soldiers in the First World War. We can also follow a chronological route along both matrilineal and patrilineal pathways to Lorna Goodison, Olive Senior, John Agard and to the Nobel laureate Derek Walcott, who recast classical mythologies within the context of the modern Caribbean.

Birds populate 'Air', as one might expect, but, counterintuitively, we find fish here too: namely in Kwame Dawes' 'Progeny of Air', which addresses the existential threat that industrial agribusiness poses to the life of a Canadian salmon. We also find flora: Denise Saul's short lyric 'Clematis' reaches, as does its titular plant, up from the mundane earth towards the heavens – while Will Harris's short-lined quatrains in 'Late Song' cast a backwards glance that counterpoints Walt Whitman when they speak of what it is 'to be alone & in / the grassing wind'.

'Water' inescapably refers us to the Black Atlantic, and with it, David Dabydeen's lyrical epic from the early 1990s, 'Turner'. Along with salt water, we have the monsoon, rivers and our relationship with them. Rain falls in a storm where Jackie Kay and her baby son transcend the language barrier in Italy to find the warmth of human shelter within the confines of a 'small madeira cake house'. Ideas of peripherality and estrangement are two resounding themes in the anthology, which, for example, we encounter in Moniza Alvi's 'At Walberswick' and Momtaza Mehri's 'At the Port'. Alternatively, we find ourselves immersed in Elizabeth-Jane Burnett's experimental take on wild urban swimming amongst the 'drone lorry / drone camera / drone dog' in 'King's Cross Pond'.

Alongside more direct representations of 'Fire', such as Nina Mingya Powles' concrete 'Volcanology', there is also the fierce remonstration of Inua Ellams' slash-punctuated paragraph 'Fuck /Humanity' which burns with rage and resistance. Jeet Thayil's 'Zoology' is a testimony to the ravages of our ongoing assault on biodiversity while Warsan Shire's tender ode to a father in 'Bless the Camels' conjures a moon that deflects the bright light of the desert sun and brings other ontological paradigms into sharper focus. As Nick Makoha reminds us in his intellectually lateral and aphoristic prose poem 'Codex', our situation is urgent: 'The furnace is the city's costume. / This world is a desperate element'.

This urgency is evident in the decline of political and ecological systems worldwide, in climate collapse and the structural fragility that these conditions engender. This precarity is experienced most disproportionately in the global south, and throughout more-than-human/animal populations, and is arguably the delicate thread in the web that connects all of these poems. Global-majority voices have been absenced from many discourses concerning nature throughout history. Ironically, nature is itself on the brink of erasure. This irony is not coincidental. The roots of the colonial project are deeply entangled in the perception of nature as a resource from which capital is to be extracted, as something that is other to us and either celebrated as numinous and pure or valued in terms of its potential efficacy, to be exploited and subdued. People of colour have been countering the effects of white supremacy as an economic and societal system for centuries. Now, as the global eco-structure starts to fracture, the reverberations are being felt by all. But the elegiac note only carries so far: as Toi Derricotte reminds us in her poem 'The Telly Cycle', 'joy is an act of resistance'.

It is in this spirit that we might encounter Anthony Vahni Capildeo's 'In Praise of Birds', which we find 'unbeautiful' and 'abounding in Old Norse,' as well as 'shitting ever / singing, above a low-rent skylight, on a diet of chips'. There is a sense of salutation, too, in the queer history unearthed in Ian Humphreys' 'Pansies', where it is impossible not to rejoice in the pointed enjambment of 'Camp compliance / trowelled thick as luvvie slap. Dick / Frankie, Larry, Charles, [...]'. There is much to savour in the linguistic agility that underpins Nisha Ramayya's restless take on the slippery encumbrance and agency of identity, where an agility of human–nature interrelations means we might simply close our eyes 'to change the weather'. Anthropologist Eduardo Kohn uses the term 'decolonising thought' for the process by which we become interlaced with the natural world which then leads to a shift in perception. This is how new conceptual tools are born and actualised. The poems in this anthology encourage such shifts, bringing something fresh and provocative to these vital conversations while positively complicating how we constitute and perceive environmental consciousness.

The etymology of 'anthology' refers us to *anthos*, 'flowers', and *logia*, 'collection'. We might think of *Nature Matters* as a bouquet: one that is more like Banksy's *Flower Thrower* than a bunch of air-freighted tulips from a cash-crop field in Kenya. Or it is more like an insistent wildflower meadow nestled unexpectedly within the confines of an industrial estate, where daffodils bloom alongside buddleia, pansies, lilies and hibiscus, and the oak stands alongside mahogany and tamarind, and the seasons in which they flourish and blossom may also be rainy or dry. Whichever form the picture takes, this anthology is a radical and vital offering, and one which we hope will have readers seeing it as we do: as a living, breathing instrument of change.

MONA ARSHI & KAREN McCARTHY WOOLF, 2025

NATURE MATTERS

EARTH

ZAFFAR KUNIAL

Foxglove Country

Sometimes I like to hide in the word
foxgloves – in the middle of *foxgloves*.
The *xgl* is hard to say, out of the England
of its harbouring word.
Alone it becomes a small tangle,
a witch's thimble, hard-to-toll bell,
elvish door to a door. *Xgl*
a place with a locked beginning
then a snag, a *gl*
like the little Englands of my grief,
a knotted dark that locks light
in *glisten, glow, glint, gleam*
and Oberon's banks of *eglantine*
which closes in on the opening
of *Gulliver* whose shrunken *gul*
says 'rose' in my fatherland.
Meanwhile, in the motherland, the *xg*
is almost the thumb of a lost mitten,
an impossible interior, deeper than forests
and further in. And deeper inland
is the gulp, the gulf, the gap, the grip
that goes before *love.*

KEI MILLER
Unsettled

So consider an unsettled island.
Inside – the unflattened and unsugared

fields; inside – a tegareg
sprawl of roots and canopies,

inside – the tall sentries of blood-
wood and yoke-wood and sweet-wood,

of dog-wood, of bullet trees so hard
they will one day splinter cutlasses,

will one day swing low the carcasses
of slaves; inside – a crawling

brawl of vines, unseemly
flowers that blossom from their spines;

inside – the leh-guh orchids and labrishing
hibiscuses that throw raucous

syllables at crows whose heads are red
as annattos; inside – malarial mosquitoes

that rise from stagnant ponds;
inside – a green humidity thick as mud;

inside – the stinging spurge, the night-
shades, the Madame Fates;

inside – spiders, gnats and bees,
wasps and lice and fleas; inside –

the dengue, the hookworm, the heat
and botheration; unchecked macka

sharp as crucifixion. This is no paradise –
not yet – not this unfriendly, untamed island –

this unsanitised, unstructured island –
this unmannered, unmeasured island;

this island: unwritten, unsettled, unmapped.

VICTORIA ADUKWEI BULLEY
Of the Snail & its Loveliness

1.

Once, I saw a snail so small
so young its shell was still
        transparent.

I stopped to look – I had the time
to see a thing unseen before –
        a tiny flute

a ghost of white that swayed
        within the sleeping shell,
marking time so faithfully.

        Little snail,
        you'll never know what happened
outside as you dreamed.

        I watched your small heart's beating
                & called my love
        to come & see.

2.

Nomad of no fixed address, praise
your paradox, your calcium elasticity.
You who wander are not lost.
Home is wherever you are right now.
Everywhere you go is where you live.

3.

Let me sing of the snail
          & its loveliness, of the beauty
I have ruined underfoot,
          wincing as though the pain
were entirely mine.
          Knowing I could walk this city
in a fatal rush
          I have learned to step aside for you.
Have crouched, even, in the rain
          to move you further along your way
in the line of your direction.
          & what is care but this: to hold
that which comes too soon to harm
          & set it on a safer path.
To say *I'm sorry*, simply –
          to do this, & not dance.
To signal the way to that place
          where the skin meets itself again
or failing that, where honey
          fills the wound's red mouth;
solders a space left empty
          of love. *Love*,
this way, we might say,
          this way,
holding, sometimes, the other
          sometimes the lonely self
until it can be said, *love*,
          we are home now.

ANDRE BAGOO

Untouched

In this savannah,
            trees have walked
    away, leaving an expanse
                of green loneliness in which
    you crawl and creep, each of
                your limbs like one of the boys
    who almost loved me: bashful,
                sensitive, afraid, leaves opening
only by the night, thorny, purple-
                flowered, strong-stemmed: Ti
    Marie, Misé Marie, morivivi,
                touch-me-not, shame plant,
    Mary Shut Your Door. Each
                leaf, each name, the same
    lover, spread in poor soil,
                where once cane was
    grown and slaves knew.

MALIKA BOOKER

Songs of Mahogany

1.

And then I realised the whole house was filled with mahogany, the doorknobs,
the banisters, the stairs themselves . . .
it was worship and annihilation all in one.

2.

I was compelled to assist in cutting a great deal of Mahogany
wood, writes Olaudah Equiano. Think of the mornings he toiled
and toiled to capture swirling grains of the tree crotch, under

the tyranny of mosquitos. Think of his back breaking, while
harvesting rows of trunks bigger than the big house, to harness,
then tumble into nearby river water. Logs lashed

together, lumbering, riding currents towards their first
destination, a main port, to be buried in the belly of ships. Think
genocide visited here and men laboured in the art of such a thing.
Speak of Mahogany. O speak of the people of the land!

3.

Speak of Mahogany. Speak
of the original people of the land!
And think of   bodies/   bodies/   blood/
   black/ blessed/ bones/ back/ back broad/
         borders/ broken branches/
broken bough/ brown/   bleed/   balsam/
            balm/   breathless/

Here is a space of interruption,
where hands slap wooden surfaces
for luck and palms lick wood for praise.
This is how Noah came to bend ancient
mahogany bones into a skeletal spine
for his ark, while Jamaican crows cra cra.
How they came to revere the mahogany,
whose demise summoned the jabbering crows.

4.

When Chippendale said *silky mahogany was a sensory delight*,
did he know that its music would be a relentless history, where
     blues
lick wood and the earth chants down Babylon, blam blam blam
they fall and fall and fall, till forty years later the rich red trunks
are legend, a mythical fancy wood, *Drop them one by one –*
Go lang boy! Then dip them dip them, but there is no healing
stream. Their majestic shadows opulent in these country houses.

5.

Genocide visited here, as men laboured in the art of such a thing.
Speak of Mahogany. O speak of the people of the land,
who languished in dark desolate valleys. Look yonder
into a vault where their hallowed history is buried
by architects of deceit,

          whose reckless temerity cannot subdue
          sunlight leaking fragments,
tales of men touching trunks, murmuring prayers, heads bowed
asking forgiveness, yea asking permission, before
they began to saw the flanks.

          See Noah – drawing and measuring
          while nightingales perch in branches singing.

Take note, there are Jamaican Nightingales in the orange trees
     and think
of the men condemned to chop them down, branded
             with the master's initials on their chests. Men
             who sprinkled precious water to appease.
And think again of Noah drawing and measuring, like he making war
ship, naval
     – while watching sky feeling in he bones, hurricane coming.

6.

Dusk here reeks with the gestation of mosquitoes and slithering
snakes, lizards scuttle, and insects crawl out of the forest foliage,
littered with scorpions, centipedes and towering trees. Unruly
vegetation to be gutted, scaled back, then there are the bodies
bent backs, in sun, raised machetes cutting, while monkeys
gibber flinging their bodies from limb to limb on the brown
     boughs.
Prospectors came, found shady canopies populated by the
     ancients
they slashed and burnt to plant cane, shipping severed trunks
and limbs home to the motherland. And the forests became
     graveyards.
It was the dark of this place these adventurers feared, so
     genocide visited
here, as men laboured in the art of such a thing.
Speak of Mahogany. O speak of the people of the land.

7.

In Jamaica in the big house, the house girl is on her knees
polishing the wood floor with coconut oil and orange halves.
In England servants kneel with linseed and brick dust,
worshiping this majestic red, genuflecting.

In the kitchen cook prepares the tea tray for Master. It too
is fancy wood. She walks through the house to deliver
to a man hunched over a desk shaping his will. Now think
of Brodsworth, of the old Mahogany water closet, and over
there the Spanish Mahogany dinner wagon. The balusters
added to the principal staircase and the exquisite tables
for tea drinking rituals with precise accoutrements. Peter inviting
guests to join him 'Round the Mahogany.' Thellusson hunched
over his red oak desk writing his will, casting lots for eggs
that may not hatch for generations, listening for cook's footsteps.
his tale ends and begins here. A man hunched over a desk,
inheritance, a male marking territory as the tall clock case holds
the round moon shaped face and time spreads herself out.

8.

They buried us in the belly of these ships.
Mornings we toiled and toiled
bodies and brooding, timber and cut down.

In some ways the tragedy has a silent
crescendo, somewhat operatic, somewhat
reminiscent of a dark forest.

How to cut a pomegranate

'Never,' said my father,
'Never cut a pomegranate
through the heart. It will weep blood.
Treat it delicately, with respect.

Just slit the upper skin across four quarters.
This is a magic fruit,
so when you split it open, be prepared
for the jewels of the world to tumble out,
more precious than garnets,
more lustrous than rubies,
lit as if from inside.
Each jewel contains a living seed.
Separate one crystal.
Hold it up to catch the light.
Inside is a whole universe.
No common jewel can give you this.'

Afterwards, I tried to make necklaces
of pomegranate seeds.
The juice spurted out, bright crimson,
and stained my fingers, then my mouth.

I didn't mind. The juice tasted of gardens
I had never seen, voluptuous
with myrtle, lemon, jasmine,
and alive with parrots' wings.

The pomegranate reminded me
that somewhere I had another home.

HANNAH LOWE

The Trees

In the pebbledash houses
on streets in this city
we're sleeping so thoroughly
sunk in the fog of our beds
so nobody hears the last word of the oak or the elm
what the cherry tree said
or the creak or the thud as they fall
and nobody that sees the trickle of sap

is actually blood.
But just before sunrise,
the ravens fly up
like a cutaway shot in a movie
where something too awful
has happened to watch it head on –
whatever's been done by the man
with the knife or the gun or the bomb.

ALYCIA PIRMOHAMED
Elegy with Two Elk and a Compass

In Jasper, Alberta, I pass through the widowed poplars.
Evening hikes up its dark hems, trees begin howling their elegies,
when loosened from the thicket, two elk walk into my gaze.

Here, in the gap between needle point and destination,
there is an unkind earth that persists even as loss petals down
leaving the poplars bare. Earlier that day, I had crossed
the forest's bridges and stepped beyond its corridors.

I had longed to find the hidden trail that led to the valley of roses.

From the elk, I am expecting a lesson, as if Allah has
        approached me
in the shape of a compass built from antler and vine.
Their muscles tense. One rises into a gallop, widening the field.

Its legs seize with strength and I remain in the space left behind:
the sudden nakedness of a northern forest. I am unable to follow—
The elk, in their way, have mastered living by mastering
        letting go.
Soon it will rain, and we will all wear our haloes of mist.

Tree of the Invisible Man

I can say nothing of its name, save the name
of the factory behind which it stood, the one bleeding
dyes all day, making gutters that once were streams
a carnival of bright death – green, red: Golden

Textiles. The tree itself was a lesson in the art
of contortion, its hard angles an eloquent semaphore,
clear lines of survival under abuse. It had a hole
right through its trunk. First we peeked through it,

but months later we stopped, only to see who could
        make a matching chink
           through cellulose
      – that narrow
    body. I see its shape now as I close my eyes, the seven
punctures we managed to riddle it with, the pens it cost us,

coat hangers, twisted forks, a stolen corkscrew, the pale
gleam of those offerings at its base when the sun set;
the view through the gaps if you stepped back – squinted,
as though the eight holes were one, no bark between.

Its dark roughness is the skin I inhabit in this dream
where I'm away from home, visible as a threat, unnoticed
though breathing. I count the bullets shot by ganged boys
in blue, measure their circumference against my skin:

calibre, quantity per dark double, drawing a map of round
        fissures where my flesh should be,
      flood of projectiles at my feet. The view

　　　　　clears as I squint,
my reflection shines
　　　　like water at sunset.
The whole widens.
　　　　　　　　One night, I am all mirror – no flesh.

BENJAMIN ZEPHANIAH

Nature Trail

At the bottom of my garden
There's a hedgehog and a frog
And a lot of creepy-crawlies
Living underneath a log.
There's a baby daddy long legs
And an easy-going snail
And a family of woodlice.
All are on my nature trail.

There are caterpillars waiting
For their time to come to fly.
There are worms turning the earth over
As ladybirds fly by,
Birds will visit, cats will visit
But they always chose their time
And I've even seen a fox visit
This wild garden of mine.

Squirrels come to nick my nuts
And busy bees come buzzing
And when the night time comes
Sometimes some dragonflies come humming,
My garden mice are very shy
And I've seen bats that growl
And in my garden I have seen
A very wise old owl.

My garden is a lively place
There's always something happening,
There's this constant search for food

And then there's all that flowering,
When you have a garden
You will never be alone
And I believe we all deserve
A garden of our own.

SAFIYA KAMARIA KINSHASA

If Our Tree in Manor House Gardens Could Talk

are we okay?

because when my hands smelled cobwebs obsessed
with watching hydrangea bush-headed girls float
from their beds, i saw you wearing an extra layer.
cobwebs adore watching dark things move
in the way a swan might drift down rivers barking bout
dark girls floating too fast, they move like they can pass
through walls & arrogant things: 'deceit' for example.
i thought you would have stayed warm a little longer,
that extra polyester layer didn't even look warm
i think you were just trying to warn me winter
was coming earlier than expected, when it came
people with Aldi bags tried to teeth the lake as it slept,
cowards . . .

                    i'm asking politely & not so politely,
my arms landed in the uplift, you thought i was protesting
but i wasn't you thought i was living but that wasn't,
foolish, you do this a lot you make assumptions
when you ain't bothered to get to know the real me.
the protest was boring, no one did anything with elephants,
while it all went down a couple daisies made a pact,
they said they would bloom early cause everything
is coming early, now when they wake up nothing
will be there to breathe dynamite down their throats,
it's a shame, it's a damn shame we don't all work together,
what is the point of having everything
then doing nothing with it?

          i am not asking you to shoot upwards
& suffer the consequences, my stretch marks left
an imprint on your cheek like cake frosting,
you peeped inside me, found a baby bird whimpering,
unusual for me yet normal for your kind you assumed
it needed flight lessons, not food not water but clouds
confined to blues, not everything enjoys being engulfed,
you watched the banks rising & didn't give a damn
because strength does not need support, strength can
build its own bridges, strength can replenish itself
after fires it didn't start. the living are being stripped
before you & you still believe carving yourself in me
will make it better,

SUJATA BHATT

શેરડી (Shérdi)

The way I learned
to eat sugar cane in Sanosra:
I use my teeth
to tear the outer hard *chaal*
then, bite off strips
of the white fibrous heart –
suck hard with my teeth, press down
and the juice spills out.

January mornings
the farmer cuts tender green sugar cane
and brings it to our door.
Afternoon, when the elders are asleep
we sneak outside carrying the long smooth stalks.
The sun warms us, the dogs yawn,
our teeth grow strong
our jaws are numb;
for hours we suck out the *russ*, the juice
       sticky all over our hands

So tonight
when you tell me to use my teeth,
to suck hard, harder,
then, I smell sugar cane grass
    in your hair
and imagine you'd like to be
shérdi shérdi out in the fields
   the stalks sway
     opening a path before us

Neopet

—it's a circle, right? Virtual pet websites are about wealth
accumulation. Wealth accumulation is about class. Class
is about domination, and domination, of course, is about
popular consensus. Popularity is about currency. Currency is
points. Points are about buying commodities. Commodities
are weapons and armour and property and paint-brushes.
Paintbrushes are about customising your Neopet to look like
a wizard and or a gold bust or a fairy or cloud spirit, but pretty
much everyone wants a baby paintbrush. Baby paintbrushes are
about making everything really cute. And making everything
really cute is just reimagining normal stu in a palette of pastels
and puppy eyes. Puppy eyes are about maternal instinct.
Maternal instinct is about the gendered division of labour. The
division of labour is about owners and masters. Owners and
masters, even when they're six-year-olds, are about capitalism
(and its precedents). And capitalism and its precedents are
about wealth accumulation, which brings me back to—

TISHANI DOSHI

De-extinction Postcard

I have spent so many nights
worrying about losing bones, teeth,
hair, recovering a ring of tanzanite. As a child
I wanted to be a dinosaur, roaming the floodplains—
duck-billed, stout. Having survived, I would like to pull
carcasses out of sinkholes and set them to work, *Run,*
Spinosaurus, run! The problem with resurrections is there is still
all this life—unexplained bulbs in the flower beds, cabbage heads,
mud, mosquitoes foraging at dusk to smother all our celestial
striving. I'd miss bananas. I'd miss melancholy. Lazarus limped
home but we know nothing of what happened in the soundless
dark—only the rise, only the returning. I'm trying to hold
this late morning, these parched yellow flowers,
even the two dogs at my feet, synching heartbeats,
who do not once consider the tragedy
of a day continuing without them—
                    To whomsoever this should reach:
I write from a town that no longer exists,
in a language whose final words have been carved
into a trunk of pylon. Send no rescue missions
for us. If you have known love, you understand,
the view to infinity is marred by hedgerow,
a line of bedclothes drying. The going,
when it goes, is forever gone.

duplex i

we must begin again   the repeating
chorus an echo calling   an ending

      the chorus sings   the note echoes ending
      the grave is still a bleeding wound   a womb

the grave   the still bleeding wound   and the womb
of us all   this earth that would bring us back

      and all of this to earth would bring us back
      to itself   a more wanting creation

we ourselves   are here   wanting creation
to make something new or to make something

      at all   we make new things that mean nothing
      at all   there is nothing that cures empty

there is nothing at all that fills empty
you must begin again   again   again

ISHION HUTCHINSON
from *School of Instructions*

They shovelled the long trenches day and night.

Frostbitten mud. Shellshock mud. Dungheap mud. Imperial mud.
Venereal mud. Malaria mud. Hun bait mud. Mating mud.
1655 mud: white flashes of sharks. Golgotha mud. Chilblain mud.
Caliban mud. Cannibal mud. Ha ha ha mud. Amnesia mud.
Drapetomania mud. Lice mud. Pyrexia mud. Exposure mud.
    Aphasia mud.
No-man's-land's-Everyman's mud. And the smoking flax mud.
Dysentery mud. Septic sore mud. Hogpen mud. Nephritis mud.
Constipated mud. Faith mud. Sandfly fever mud. Rat mud.
Sheol mud. Ir-ha-cheres mud. Ague mud. Asquith mud. Parade
    mud.
Scabies mud. Mumps mud. Memra mud. Pneumonia mud.
Mene mene tekel upharsin mud. Civil war mud.
And darkness and worms will be their dwelling place mud.
Yaws mud. Gog mud. Magog mud. God mud.
Canaan the unseen, as promised, saw mud.

They resurrected new counterkingdoms,
by the arbitrament of the sword mud.

from *Faust*

vi.

Kernels of rain   or *seeds* of rain
     is how raindrops translate

so that even the rain is not itself
                 when you wait mouth open
                 looking sceptical or just pulling
                 at the dry earth with broken lips.

Who will plant the rain   in a hearse so that the moon blooms
                             from his heart?
Grandfather, laid out and burnt like a stoic length of chaff,
his mind a prophecy of smoke.
    Two rupees in his breast pocket and a slip of white, neatly folded,
       with his son's address on it.

Smoke that is not rain nor wheat but leans
into them both like a fever
unmatched by the living.

There   he says, in a blue of white,
that is all you ever needed to know about wheat.

xiii.

The grain as hands   her hands as grain
The grain as light   dust as grain
As light as dust   her hands as seed
Grain as weather   as moving through
The earth where   grain falls she falls
Here as water   sweetened after a fast
The grain she saw   growing not as grain
Is your father   in the marketplace
Grain cursed   penniless, auctioned
Shuffling home   unseasonable yields
Indelible shame   and hunger its own
shame sets fire to   grain plots a loss
standing over a   jute sack of seed
that is his body   and they appraise it
between fingers   for the going rate
father if I could   have bought a year
of wheat exchanged   for bread you'd
stride powerfully   as a boy as grain
in the hands of   a mother regained
from the earth   where she fell into
Bitter yellow   rattle light this chance
harvest

Pansies

The Wild Pansy can be found anywhere
the ground has been disturbed.
They flower once, seed and die off.
Pansies Quarterly (Autumn Issue, 1970)

I still adore them even though
we really shouldn't – the old guard
from the sixties and seventies. Those
confirmed bachelors who played fey.
Sharpened pennies tossed to the crowd
from pursed lips. Laugh at me, Duckie
not with me. Camp compliance
trowelled thick as luvvie slap. Dick
Frankie, Larry, Charles, Mr Humphries
Kenneth's *What's the bloody point?*
Cilla's confidante upstairs at The Black Cap
who didn't like Pride, preferred sex
when it was illegal. *I dunno, hun*
it just felt dirty, thrilling back then.

JASON ALLEN-PAISANT
Daffodils
(Speculation on Future Blackness)

It's time to write about daffodils
again to hear

a different sound
from the word

daffodil

Imagine daffodils in the corner
of a sound system

in Clapham
Can't you?

Well you must
try to imagine daffodils

in the hands of a black family
on a black walk

in spring

AIR

ANTHONY VAHNI CAPILDEO
In Praise of Birds

In praise of high-contrast birds, purple bougainvillea
thicketing the golden oriole.

In praise of civic birds, vultures cleansing the valleys,
hummingbird logos on the tails of propeller planes; in praise
of adaptable birds, the herring gull that demonstrates its
knowledge of how to use a box junction, and seems to want
to cross the road.

In praise of birds eaten by aeroplane engines; in praise of
birds trained to hunt drones; in praise of birds that, having
nothing to do with human processes, crash aeroplanes.

In praise of suicidal birds, brown ground doves forgetful of
wingèdness, in front of cars, slowly crossing the road.

In praise of perse birds like fish smashing out of a bowl.

In praise of talk being cheep, and in praise of men who shut
up about birds.

In praise of birds of death and communication, Garuda
the almost-but-more-than-an-eagle vehicle of the darkly
bejewelled and awfully laughing Lord of Death.

In praise of badly drawn birds.

In praise of white egrets, sitting on mud, hippos, and lines
about old age.

In praise of Old English birds of exile, the gannet's laughter,
swathes of remembered seabirds booming and chuckling,
the urgent cuckoo blazing on about summer, mournful
and mindblowing, driving the sailor over the edge towards
impossible targets, scornful of gardens, salty about city life – I
can't stand not setting off; far is seldom far enough.

In praise of a turn of good cluck.

In praise of the high-dancing birds carried on the heads of
masqueraders and built by wirebenders to carry the spirit of
an archipelago of more than seven thousand isles.

In praise of grackles quarrelling on the lawn.

In praise of unbeautiful birds abounding in Old Norse,
language of scavenging ravens, thought and memory, a
treacherous duo. The giantess down from the mountain
complained – I couldn't sleep in a coastal bed because of the
yammering of waterfowl. Every morning that blasted seagull
wakes me.

In praise of the peacocks invading the car park at the Viking
conference in York, warming their spread tails on the bodies
of cars.

In praise of the early bird who liberates the dewy worm from
glaucous grass.

In praise of birds of timetelling: green-rumped parrots for
morning, kiskadees dipping at night: and the absence of birds
of timetelling, the unreeled horror of humanly meaningless
time.

In praise of the bird of the soul that flies out when the body is molested, and in praise of that bird recalling the abuse room as if perched on the highest point of the pinewood press.
In praise of the blueblack grassquit, which is inky and small.
In praise of the albatross, in praise of the double doors to a swimming baths hall.
In praise of birds of concussion, notes in the air being all the brain can cope with.

In praise of birds as edible and in praise of birds as angels and in praise of birds as stones and in praise of Thoth the Ibis.

In praise of the birds of climate change, forest warblers bringing a new song to the suburbs, late-leaving Arctic tern teenagers blizzarding the beach.

In praise of ducking and diving, and without praise of the cruelty of quills.

In praise of birds that are not punctuation, that are not calendars, that are not words.

In praise of birds that occupy and disrupt a lyrical musical staff.

In praise of birds that singing still do shit, shitting ever singing, above a low-rent skylight, on a diet of chips.

In praise of triangulation and three unseen corncrakes by whose calls guests may recognize the way to the house on the tipsy hill.

In praise of increasingly grotesque fossil remains of proto-birds, and the discovery of normality as never having been such.

In praise of birds plucked for dream armour, flame fur, plate plume, and in praise of women who fight like cranes and swans.

In praise of thump and slime.

In praise of fine feathers, prophecies, and export regulations.

In praise of Quetzalcoatl. Tremble to say more.

In praise of the birds of prognostication, gutted, magnetic, or altering their calls.
In praise of rare and less showy doctors refraining from labelling immigrants as insane or aggressive, as more regularly spotted doctors may be observed to do.
In praise of Suibhne, driven mad by the dinning of church bells, yearning for his dinner of unchlorinated cress.
In praise of Suibhne's flights crossing land and water, and Suibhne's poetry crossing time and language, to and from, tidalectic, praise.

DENISE SAUL

Clematis

Whose firmament do they look up to
when foretelling Surrey weather?
They cling to what was never theirs
and yet the crowns are rewarded with
delicate things of solemn purple.
Unlike vine suffered to dry
on the iron fence, clematis clings
to bricks and rinse of sunlight.
Thankless they insist that the earth is theirs.

We Are the Forests and They Are the Lions

At this hour, the river (where it starts) emits ice flowers. They
are creamy and geometric. On the windshield, my pass for
Lory State Park, where a runner strangled a panther last week,
snapping its neck when it pounced, is peeling off. I think of the
day we wandered, waist high, through the tangles of lime yellow
brush above the thick pink earth of the shore. All this mud
and red and green, every day. All these years in Colorado, and
I haven't pierced belonging beyond my strong, fine feeling of
connection with the people around me. Perhaps that's right. It's
late, snowing, and the viral load of a recent illness is still moving
through. Tomorrow is a political holiday. All over the country
people are gathering to protest the Emergency. Tea, then we'll
drive to the protest with empty stomachs. You need a car or a
truck in the West. The full moon stops us from thinking. My
son is washing the dishes on the last day of childhood. The rose
on my shrine is a reminder to remain vertical, to keep grading
papers. I feel weirdly hopeful. A writer I barely know wrote, after
many years, to ask if she could forward our brief collaboration to
a chapbook press. I said no. Another poet sent a text about ants,
and another poet called me. In the background of our video
call, I could see the blobby violet Michigan dusk. Somehow, I
finished grading twenty-five essays. My mother massaged my
head with coconut oil because my eyes, in their sockets, ached.
Do eyes have stems? I think of the blossoming that happens
every day. Because it was snowing, I gave my students an
optional assignment to extend a snowball to someone else, a
gift, with as much tenderness or presence as they could muster.
The only other thing I want to say about this day is that, at one
point, I leaned back and pulled an English translation of the
Mahabharat off the shelf. A bed-time story, my mother stroking

my hair in Hayes, the book was only, ever, verbal, a caution
or promise as the sun fell out of the sky. 'We are the forest,' I
repeat, my fingertip below the line. I recall my uncle's story of
encountering a lion in the jungle above Rishikesh. His teacher
ran away. The other apprentice ran away. My uncle, who was
blind and could not run, stood very still. 'And then,' he said, in
the English that he had, 'the lion walked through me.' Do you
believe you can rearrange your molecules so that the threat (a
mouth of ragged teeth) could go right through the space you
were or had to be? See: Keanu Reeves. No, don't.

DZIFA BENSON
Complaint to a Flambouyant

Big tree, Mother tree. Flamed
long breather, deepest of time's thinkers—

in this small savannah sliced out of the city
a chicken scratches at an anthill and soon

finds the bones of its mother's thigh.
This crimson wound of saliva and dust

is the mouth from which I am speaking
in your language of carbon, sap and distress signals.

Our attempts to smudge out the sky
is a truth as dark as the cosmos and how long

we have carried our hearts outside our bodies
across your orange-red horizons, breaking

everything that is meant to hold us.
Maybe you listen for nothing more than

the frequencies of whisperings in your highest
boughs during your journeys of breath

in our solar plexus but we never hear
you complain about losing your leaves even

as your beauty flares like fat, jubilant bells.
If only we were greener things with roots

like yours curling into the forest floor as we stare
up at the palm-nut vulture gliding on thermals.

RUSHIKA WICK

Gaia in the Live Lounge
(COVID 19 Pandemic 2020)

I am driving to see my mother
playing lottery with a small chance
of killing her there are so many ways of
killing by love and this is just one version
I think of monogamists in perfect kitchens
letting the water run out of modern taps
and soft kittens crushed by children
and people who feed ducks with supermarket bread
when the sun shines and female bodies
limp on the floor and I think that maybe
the worst of all these sad things
is killing your mother because
there is no greater location of love

that is love's first home
unspoken or full-sung mother is the sky
above your head and cracking panes
of thin glass and cold water and fever
a flock of swifts flew over my car turning
a page and the sky was
cornflower-blue tinged with dazzling violet
and the air was clean with spring
and I felt the terrifying sign of earth's power
and how she had tolerated my near killing of her
until she'd had enough and turned
knowing that it is worse to raise murderers

Scale

The map reveals
so many stars –
two constellations
in the shape of bears,
a peacock, Pavo,
in the southern hemisphere,
the spaces between galaxies,
the emptiness,
the not-quite emptiness
it doesn't show,
the single
atom
H
in every cubic meter –
the atom
that is
not quite
still –
how cold it is
between the galaxies,
the snowdrops in the garden
the morning after frost.

NIDHI ZAK/ARIA EIPE
What birds plunge through
is not the intimate space

She can't believe this jag-winged majesty
really wants a piece of her

creature stealing up
                    rising like
                    a black and leafy ledge

into the honey-bearing chaos
                    of high summer.

Everyone's voice was suddenly lifted
          . . . O, but everyone was a bird!

But it isn't a bird
                    it's a man in a bird suit
                    a song inside him, blue
                    shoulders instead of feathers.

There is a sky, teeming with winged
things, birds with fiery plumage
winging wildly across the white
          orchards and dark-green fields
                              on – on – and out

of sight

a stand of white pines

                    i n d i v i d u a l flames
          against the masonry of black smoke

                         the day-blind stars
                    waiting with their light.

                              Stillness falls like a cloud.

Suddenly she puts out her wing –
the whole, full, flirtatious span of it:

                         blackbird, my lord,
                              as nothing will hurt you
                                   I'll sing as I love.

Progeny of Air

The propellers undress the sea;
the pattern of foam like a broken zip
opening where the bow cuts the wave

and closing in its wake. The seals bark.
Gulls call and dive, then soar loaded with catch.
The smell of rotting salmon lingers over the Bay

of Fundy, like a mortuary's disinfected air;
fish farms litter the coastline;
metal islands cultivating with scientific

precision these grey-black, pink-fleshed fish.
In the old days, salmon would leap up the river to spawn,
journeying against the current. They are

travellers: When tucked too low searching for
undertows to rest upon, they often scrape
their bellies on the sharp adze and bleed.

Now watch them turn and turn
in the cages waiting for the feed of
colourised herring to spit from the silver

computer bins over the islands of sea farms,
and General, the hugest of the salmon,
has a square nose where a seal chewed

on a superfreeze winter night when
her blood panicked and almost froze.
Jean Pierre, the technician and sea-cage guard,

thinks they should roast the General in onions
and fresh sea water. It is hard to read mercy
in his stare and matter-of-factly way.

He wears layers, fisherman's uniform,
passed from generation to generation:
the plaid shirt, the stained yellow jacket,

the ripped olive-green boots, the black
slack trousers with holes, the whiskers
and eye of sparkle, as if salt-sea has crystallised

on his sharp cornea. He guides the boat in;
spills us out after our visit with a grunt and grin,
willing us to wet our sneakers at the water's

edge. The sun blazes through the chill.
The motor stutters, the sea parts, and
then zips shut and still.

Stunned by their own intake of poison,
the salmon turn belly up on the surface;
then sucked up by the plastic piscalator,

they plop limp and gasping in the sunlight.
One by one the gloved technicians
press with their thumbs the underside of the fish

spilling the eggs into tiny cups
destined for the hatchery, anaesthetised eyes
glazed shock on the steel deck.

They know the males from the females:
always keep them apart, never let seed touch egg,
never let the wind carry the smell of birthing

through the June air. Unburdened now the fish
are flung back in – they twitch, then tentative
as hungover denizens of nightmares, they swim

the old sisyphean orbit of their tiny cosmos.
The fish try to spawn at night
but only fart bubbles and herring.

On the beach the rank saltiness of murdered salmon
is thick in the air. Brown seaweed sucks up the blood.
The beach is a construction site of huge cement blocks

which moor the sea-cages when tossed eighty feet down.
They sink into the muddy floor of the bay and stick.
There is no way out of this prison for the salmon,

they spin and spin in the algae-green netting,
perpetually caught in limbo, waiting for years before
being drawn up and slaughtered, steaked and stewed.

And in the morning's silence,
the sun is turning over for a last doze,
and silver startles the placid ocean.

Against the grey green of Deer Island
a salmon leaps in a magical arc,
slaps the metal walkway in a bounce,

and then dives, cutting the chilled water on the other side.
Swimming, swimming is General (this is my fantasy)
with the square nose and skin gone pink with seal bites,

escaping from this wall of nets and weed.
General swims up river alone,
leaping the current with her empty womb,

leaping, still instinct, still travelling
to the edge of Lake Utopia, where
after so many journeyings, after abandoning

this secure world of spawning and living
at the delicate hands of technicians,
after denying herself social security and

the predictability of a steady feeding
and the safety from predator seal and osprey;
after enacting the Sisyphean patterns of all fish,

here, in the shadow of the Connors Sardine Factory
she spawns her progeny of air and dies.

FRED D'AGUIAR

January

Do I mean wasps when I say –
Not this morning
Not last night
Not the company
I keep in a house that hoards me

Taken singly none could do this to me
Together they prove too much
They arrive at first light
As I doze they spread
This blanket of their

Compressed bodies on
Me so that I wake with a
Shimmer for my skin a hum
In the room and my dread about
Opening my eyes or reaching for my specs

I am boiled down to giant ears
As the colony stirs
I wish I could stay
Glued to the afternoon
Covered by bees or do I mean –

6th

I keep company with bees
Fly-bouncing off walls
My eyes latch to them
That me turned fragment
Off plate bees ziggurat

I bristle at the thought
Of a bee's caress
One inquisitive needle
From each bee
For every pore on me

Some current
Sways fine hairs
Behind neck
Backs of arms
Till they stand

It was never the mountains

Sunday service was the only exception.
Otherwise, it was better to stay inside, safer,
my parents reasoned, their fear bolt-locking the door
every Friday evening till Monday morning.
There was no exploration of the Yorkshire peaks
in my childhood, too dangerous I assumed.
Postcards offered cavernous mountains; wilderness
so rough and unforgiving it might swallow you whole.
Instead, I loved the flowers on my bedroom wallpaper,
scratched their paper petals under the Sun
of fluorescent lamp, until scrunched under my nails.

But when I was old enough to sneak out with Maz,
I met those mountains, as she screeched her first car
round country corners to declare our incoming.
A Black and a Brown girl, aliens descending
in flimsy trainers, to God's own country, though never ours.
We almost forgot the bodies we were in
till we found stares so sinister, boring into us
for answers we would never find, tiptoeing around
people avoiding or barging straight through us.
My parents' fear, ice water running through my chest.

Yet in the mountains, I discovered colossal sculptures;
summits, stretching beyond the limits of my spine
and trails, a rocky invitation to embark upon them.
I felt no judgement in the wind, only crisp air,
flowing to soothe my breathlessness, bird's eye views
unfurling a kingdom of greenery, and those same people
below, nothing more than specks in its mystery.

Wondrous peaks, holy unshakable altars,
mountains, bigger than all of us.

WILL HARRIS

Late Song

At first I turned away
to be alone & in
the grassing wind
imagined a stand of

trees seen from
the side of a passing
van, birch eyes turning
from the view itself

towards the road.
By choice, I gave this
hand to bear. We were
walking home. No

more sorry, no more
staking claim on
land or persons for
the unknown sake of

which we spent so long
in circles, raking over
the image owned
by speaking. I turned

in the wake of a bad
economy, moving
backwards, turning as
poets turn from what

it was had moved us &
in turning I could
hear our secrets being
relayed in cars &

car lights & in bright
blue signs seen
through the rain that
fell burning like

confetti. I said you
said I said. A space
emerged between
us & I turned to face

you through its
weather. Wherever
we stood, I turned
away to see you better.

NISHA RAMAYYA

we are seen by the world / what must be seen

for Edmund Hardy

if we are seen by the world
small brown birds
finding themselves
making friends with hawthorn
hedges pluck buds
twist pearl on thorn blossom
pricks christen me nancy
why didn't you name me
name me nancy
writes poetry in secret
writes about gym pants
but I never write
(bookworm promises)
(crossing fingers at the origins)
never until
 mos and myre with clot and clay will cling
 mos and myre with clot and clay will cling
 mos and myre with clot and clay will cling
never until my accent
stretches to meet the premise of these chronicles

schooled in whose chronicles my own
heart skewered in whose gardens
I watch from the window
triśūla break lilac tree
liberate leaves
like heads heads like friends

old school ties
skew the whole world
cleave what must clag
keep porridge oats in lockets
(who loves you baby)
potatoes in bigger lockets
(who stomachs you baby)
my own sweetheart
assimilation cringe
slubbering in the peel
feeling up the wall
separating instances of not
not racist and not racist but
try denting the wall the view from the window

I close my eyes
to change the weather
as moonstone must
be seen to sing with spite
lappered thick
and filthily stinked
oh dirty feet blood-clotter
oh grease monkey clod-hopper
oh cloud-devourer spit
    out the tricks of the light
    out the dreams of bookworm-in-bothy
    outwith the hawthorn hedge
spiteful the noise
made by privilege
when boiling over
mess made by ejected oats
bitter the blout
breaking off the storm

it slushes the need for change
anothering blood rush out with force

half melted snow in the booth
foul the confession
every stage is a toilet
every reading a pot
for covering sounds
sounds like pearl return to clod
like talking about difference is
gludderly work
imagine a blue-sky brocade
shawl draped across
history's jelly slub
imagine white granite scaffolding
clatty lapse reactions
time sleekit to the touch
repetition transports
I start again
at the shared oranges of poetry and myth
my lubberly and delicate
common or garden variety
skin is no admission if what must be seen

MONA ARSHI

Syllabising the Birds
(the Godwit, the Graylag Goose,
the Lapwing)

I   am   standing in the   shadow bands.

Oh wei! Kui   Thoreh   Deh Chug-

Nothing   behaves   as   it   should.

-a-teh- Rakh lai, dekh leh

The   wind bites and   language is   one   moment

Hass lai - akh-akh Thoreh-deh, thoreh-deh

a   warm   feather and   the   next

Chore! Chore! Kui!   Kui!

it   is   a   roar   in   your   ear.

A.K. RAMANUJAN

Ecology

The day after the first rain,
for years, I would come home
in a rage,

for I could see from a mile away
our three Red Champak trees
had done it again,

had burst into flower and given Mother
her first blinding migraine
of the season

with their street-long heavy-hung
yellow pollen fog of a fragrance
no wind could sift,

no door could shut out from our black-
pillared house whose walls had ears
and eyes,

scales, smells, bone-creaks, nightly
visiting voices, and were porous
like us,

but Mother, flashing her temper
like her mother's twisted silver,
grandchildren's knickers

wet as the cold pack on her head,
would not let us cut down
a flowering tree

almost as old as she, seeded,
she said, by a passing bird's
providential droppings

to give her gods and her daughters
and daughters' daughters basketfuls
of annual flower

and for one line of cousins
a dower of migraines in season.

SENI SENEVIRATNE
Lockdown at Leighton Moss

One day later, there'd have been no young woman
with purple hair greeting us in the visitor centre,
telling us how the booming bitterns could be heard
somewhere along the lower trail past Lilian's Hide.
Nervous at the sight of a man touching his face
while he stacks the coffee cups, we escape outdoors
to walk between the reed beds, bask in the wide open
as everything else is closing down. Out of the expanse

comes the low moan of the bittern's call. It echoes from
untraceable directions, lands in the pivot of my pelvis,
my centre of gravity, a grounding place amidst shifting
uncertainties. Soon enough this place will be off-limits.
But today, lost in the thrill of the bittern's mating song,
I raise my binoculars and watch a marsh harrier soar.

RAYMOND ANTROBUS

City Boy Talks to Trees

Look at that tree and write about it.
But Mimi, I don't know the name of that tree.
I can describe it but can't distinguish it; tall, brown, bursting
with leaves like a loaded wallet,
autumn's green and yellow receipts.
It is against my nature to notice the tree. Who am I
to rustle in the wind? Mimi, my best memory
of a tree is the one that grew at the back
of my mother's garden, it might've been a young oak
or a sweetgum. My mother came back from the market with rope
and asked my father to tie it around the thickest arm,
the knot was the seat for my sister and I
so we could swing. Mimi, we sat on that knot and launched
    ourselves,
held our whole face and both arms and feet against the rope
and Tarzaned into the air. That branch held us all summer,
my parents months from their second separation,
my sister a year from running away from home, calling
the house, hanging up on Mum's new boyfriend.
When I finally answered, *You know none of this is your fault?*
I sat on the staircase with a rubber pad on the receiver so I could
    listen
through hearing aids, that one bit of her voice entered me
while I stared out the window at that tree.
See, Mimi? I don't know what I'm saying, I don't know
what I'm hearing. Me?
I'm just rustling in the wind.

Hurricane Blues

langtime lovah
mi mine run pan yu all di while
an mi membah how fus time
di two a wi come een – it did seem
like two shallow likkle snakin stream
mawchin mapless hapless a galang
tru di ruggid lanscape a di awt sang

an a soh wi did a gwaan
sohtil dat fateful day
awftah di pashan a di hurricane
furdah dan imaginaeshan ar dream
wi fine wiself lay-dung pan di same bedrack
flowin now togedah as wan stream
ridin sublime tru love lavish terrain
lush an green an brite awftah di rain
shimmarin wid glittahrin eyes
glowin in di glare a di smilin sun

langtime lovah
mi feel blue fi true wen mi tink bout yu
blue like di sky lingahrin pramis af rain
in di leakin lite in di hush af a evenin twilite
wen mi membah how fus time
di two wi come een – it did seem
like a lang lang rivah dat is wide an deep

somtime wi woz silent like di langwidge a rackstone
somtime wi woodah sing wi rivah sang as wi a wine a galang
somtime wi jus cool an caam andah plenty shady tree

somtime sawfly lappin bamboo root as dem swing an sway
somtime cascadin carefree doun a steep gully bank
somtime turbulent in tempament wi flood wi bank
but weddah ebb ar flow tru rain tru drout
wi nevah stray far fram love rigid route

ole-time sweet-awt
up til now mi still cyaan andastan
ow wi get bag doun inna somuch silt an san
rackstone debri lag-jam
sohtil wi ad woz fi flow wi separet pawt
now traversin di tarrid terrain a love lanscape
runnin fram di polueshan af a cantrite awt
mi lang fi di marvelous miracle a hurricane
fi carry mi goh a meet in stream agen
lamentin mi saltid fate
sohmizin seh it too late

WATER

KAMAU BRATHWAITE

Loss of the Innocents

Who brigg that wind into our sail like out of no. where as it
    were this golden morning
give the small skiff move . so that it scroll out on
the blue lips of the water hissing at the brow . the spirit in
    the wood

rising as we lean towards the water's flank & flash & sparkle
and our land of everlasting to the leeward
Ahead – the sound of luff & glocking as we tack – the wide
    horizon

of the wild atlantic – our hearts rise up w/water's heave & ride
to Less Beholden – the SouthPoint lighthouse still ahead
There was no skid of fish that day . the sky was clear of frown

the wind's mouth shouting loudly in our ears. the plankton knock-
ing on the curving floorboards of the hull. the rudder tingling
    taut
the skipper ridin the ship ship-shape on its careen all the way
    round to Careem Corner

Where did this sudden storm come from?
the blinding rainbreak shadow on the shimmer . the thunder
    hollering along the reefs
our bobbing wood and rope and wreck upon the water?

<27 ap 2011 . 11:35pm>

MOMTAZA MEHRI

At the Port

Lose your bearings, our bodies cried out
And the sea heard. Gave its usual, frothing reply.
The harbour is a lolling tongue.
Umbilical, it extends from the city's navel,
A protrusion of activity.
The bay is too impersonal. It shivers outside us.

Why choose to be made this insignificant?
We did it, again and again.
Regular as brackish water licking the belly of an anchored ship.
Drank in the first sight of migrating birds.
Green-eyed cormorants gliding low and assured,
Teasing the slipstream.

Below us, a nest of workers.
Men grunting in the universal language of restlessness.
One drags a vessel by an entrail of rope.
A distant city shining in his eyes.
I know no better threshold to trust in.
This thrown rope, this ribboned horizon.
A sky the colour of a skinned knee.

Here, we are smaller than our usual selves.
Cheeks lashed by the wind, the shoreline our fellow captive.
We are awash with love, almost indigo with it.
What remains unsaid lies submerged.
A sediment of disappointments.
This, a measurement of what's best left hidden,
What drifts to the surface, blooming like algae.
What can be dragged from one brink to another,
Still carrying its scent.

OLUWASEUN OLAYIWOLA
Strange Beach

I pretend I can see them,
           the disappearances,
the transparent doors. No
           one notices. Or
everyone
has noticed already,
           the shadow-green
uptwists of bear's breeches

through the earth, upside
           down, the white
willow's
leaves incandescent, arcing
           to the ground their
chlorophyll techniques
           of low-wind
forgetting,
their shuffling, light:
darkness

we cannot look away from,
           every degree of day
casting
gleam's ache down here,
over
           the sanded world—

If only I could   take you
           there, into time's
perfectly

withered manipulations,
            into the river's black-
breath
unfolding its rope between
            vision's keylock
and the plumes of
delinquent
            smoke so swelled
they are by-now simply

air. The white willows struck
long
            after the rain cedes—I
tug a leaf from the branch,
            witness a new one
already growing in its place.
            Who could call this
beauty.
The filling-in of loss,
            like a mound of
oedematous
leaf-rot, keeping us
inconsolable
            and alive—

Do not touch me now
            —unless you
mean me
to open, open farther than
            this beach and what
we endured here, has
already
            opened me—Is it that
you think

I'd rather be anything else,
        that we were gifted
the option to be anything
            more, than
temporary.

DAVID DABYDEEN

Turner I

Stillborn from all the signs. First a woman sobs
Above the creak of timbers and the cleaving
Of the sea, sobs from the depths of true
Hurt and grief, as you will never hear
But from woman giving birth, belly
Blown and flapping loose and torn like sails,
Rough sailors' hands jerking and tugging
At ropes of veins, to no avail. Blood vessels
Burst asunder, all below – deck are drowned.
Afterwards, stillness, but for the murmuring
Of women. The ship, anchored in compassion
And for profit's sake (what well-bred captain
Can resist the call of his helpless
Concubine, or the prospect of a natural
Increase in cargo?), sets sail again,
The part – born, sometimes with its mother,
Tossed overboard. Such was my bounty
Delivered so unexpectedly that at first
I could not believe this miracle of fate,
This longed-for gift of motherhood.
What was deemed mere food for sharks will become
My fable. I named it Turner
As I have given fresh names to birds and fish
And humankind, all things living but unknown,
Dimly recalled, or dead.

E. A. MARKHAM
The Sea

It used to be at the bottom of the hill
and brought white ships and news
of a far land where half my life
was scheduled to be lived.

That was at least half a life ago
of managing without maps, plans, permanence
of a dozen or more addresses
of riding the trains like a vagrant.

Today, I have visitors. They come
long distances overland. They will be uneasy
and console me for loss of the sea.
I will discourage them.

JOHN AGARD

I Am the Oak That Became a Ship

Hearts of oak our ships
Hearts of oak our men,
We always are ready, steady boys, steady,
To charge and conquer again and again.
REVEREND RYLANCE, Anthem of British Navy, 1809

Of my flesh and bone
was made Europe's first boat
to enter a world
they would call New –
a world away from acorns
and winter's white hold.
I helped extend Europe's arm
as those Vikings well knew
and Nelson too.

Anchored to woodland
  and forest-bed
    I saw myself felled –
      my limbs ship-shaped
        for water's swell –
          my arms un-draped –
            no glimmer of squirrel –
              my tarred veins sea-ready.
The tide calling out my name.

I Oak – a fallen god
finding a new way to leap.
    And so my ribs set sail
      my cleft skin braved the deep –
        mistletoe, a forgotten touch.

My now dolphin body
brought horizons closer
till the globe was a purse
and conscience fell to sleep.

At Walberswick

Ferrying, ferrying.
The weathered posts and moorings,
the white van on the bank,
a herring gull with its wings outstretched
against a strangely blue cloud.
The ferrymen of the past
and their eager dogs, they're here too.
And the circus elephants who did or didn't
cross by ferry, depending on the story.
Did they finally wade across the Blyth?
They're standing on the bank, refusing
to be separated.

When does an Indian or African elephant
become an English elephant? Does it ever?
The water is smooth and gleaming at the bank –
the choppier waves are in the middle.
I'm eternally moored and unmoored.
This ferrying, the rhythmic setting out,
the reaching the other side – and returning.

It's a fearful thing to make a gash
in timelessness.

ROGER ROBINSON

The City Kids See the Sea

For many the first time;
these kids of the tower block
and tarred playgrounds

now running towards this scene
of sea with its blended blue sky
and wave breaks of silver-tipped froth.

Most don't even bother
to take off their shoes
or roll up their trousers,

instead they run right in,
splashing each other
with arcs and sprays of delight.

Sunlight threading gold
along the sea's rippling
swells all around them

till the sea became the colour of smoke
and the sky lead; hijabs drip
and Nikes squelch back to the bus.

O city children you are as ancient
as water, as warm as the evening sun,
as calm as the tide slowly pulling away.

SHIVANEE RAMLOCHAN

Dear Husband, By the Time You Read This Letter I Will Have Already Poisoned You Dead

you flinch like a demon when you come. I irradiate
the basin of my womb
so no occupants will siege me   in the blue
harbour your ships float like gongs

                              what does it mean when men
fall out of the empty pocket of the night and take every one of our
daughters down to the surf, pressing the blades of their lips to our
cheeks til the spray runs coral pink, runs redder than feathers

you writhe in the heat and the fever of this world
makes you mad   makes you undone   and the days
pass
in flocks of orchids ground beneath white heels
in cups of perfume sucked
from each petal's broken mouth   since you came
with your brass ships the waters run counter to their purposes,
grit in the eyes of all creatures
blinded by your light. and it has been done this way when we

called the land ███
and it has been done this way
when we called the land ███
and it has been done this
way when the land called us █ called us █ called us █

how you scrape and scrape at the
blue bowl of my womb til it knocks hollow in the gloaming,

rinsing itself out in feathers that
shine
when
you captured me i was sixteen and my heart was as loud as the

waterfalls
in this last place your ships touched. fighting you the first night, i
heard the whale's teeth in my
mother's necklace grind,
                                                    echoing in the silent maritime, pulling a
velvet boneyard over me.

i have killed more in me daily than you could ever try to sow.

while you sleep, we
have set poinciana flames to all your ships now, melting the
dread iron plumage gold.
See how everything glistens, husband, in this place that never
turned your empire. Lift
up your head if you can. Great-great-
great-and-terrible-grandson of columbus, flower
your last breath. Everything you made is leaving the island.
Look how trueness returns.
How treasure turns its heart back in the waters of whales, the
silent antlerfall of that final hunt.

you made no children here.

on the causeway to hell,
                                        blame only yourself as
hummingbirds prick out your
                                        tongue.

ROY McFARLANE

Living by Troubled Waters #1

River Mumma is said to live at the fountainhead of large rivers,
where she sits on a rock combing her hair with a golden comb.
JAMAICAN FOLKLORE

My mother – the mother who would later adopt me – lived a gulley and dirt-track away from the river she was born beside. The river she walked to early in the morning as a child to draw water. The river where she sat on stones and played whilst River Mumma watched over her. Here, my mother learned of red rivers that flowed within and out of her in times of seasons. In quiet times she bathed and combed the black Indian roots of her hair. Behind dark bushes, dark eyes poured their desire all over her, unwanted desire that burst within her and over river banks, River Mumma cried. In times of swelling, rivers burst from her womb with a man child, a man child she gave to her mother. My mother returned to the river, to be baptised for the sins before and after. The same river watered the lanp she was tied to, worked hard during the day and prayed all night for a blessing. River Mumma brought her a gift – a good man who walked out of the river, to share bread and God's words on Sundays. The river that released her and allowed her to cross over when she got married, the river she cried into when her man left to go to England, the river she left to travel a thousand miles to be with her man. My mother nearly drowned in the *Rivers of Blood* speech, she knew rivers of hate that flowed along streets, out of backyards and factories. Prayed for the parting of waters to walk on dry land or the strength to walk on water but she left that to Moses and Jesus. Made a home by those troubled waters, found a child in those waters and made a home strong in love.

River Mumma still
watches over her. Waters
still run deep wherever she goes.

Small Questions Asked by the Fat Black Woman

Will the rains
cleanse the earth of shrapnel
and wasted shells

will the seas
toss up bright fish
in wave on wave of toxic shoal

will the waters
seep the shore

feeding slowly the greying
angry roots

will trees bear fruit

will I like Eve
be tempted once again
if I survive

ELIZABETH-JANE BURNETT

King's Cross Pond

*The installation aims to make us think about the relationship
between nature and the urban environment – the permanence
of buildings and the changing nature of undeveloped spaces.*
                    KING'S CROSS POND CLUB

    drone lorry
    drone camera
    drone dog   tired air too early to

swim on the train
    on the tube
    on the platform blackberries / bougainvillea

swim in armpits
    in pheromones
    in bad suits / manners   folded sports news

getting to work
getting to WORK
by all means necessary – shove it blast it knock it shake it get it to
    WORK

           I float. Small intimate pool of
strangers floating, chattering, buzzing. I float. Small intimate
likeminded lunatics. We float. Cold, cold in the bones of the
morning are stretching, are pulling out slouch, are cold in the
morning of bones getting the body to WORK in the morning

is small. A kidney of water in the city, flat and still inside cement,
DRY TARMAC, a lift going up, a train pulling across as I'm pulling
across, a dragonfly, a buttercup still inside the building of a city

is finding its rhythm and feeling the body respond, become more of itself, because it is designed to move and is doing so. More and more it is its constituent parts – particular muscles, the pulse of the heart, the feet webbing, the eyes processing peeling the cells remembering storing and labelling this – plant; this – temperature; this – day, as a good one

rung out, slipped back, rejoin the upright. They are busy and loud and private. I am light and waterlilies. They stare. I am luminous. Goldfish. I flash and flare. And so they will have something to say when they get into work, 'and there it was, this goldfish, walking down the street,' flash flash a little live splash in the street in the fleet city drone.

RANJIT HOSKOTE

Catapult

for Joy Goswami

Blindfold the boatman rows
       his sampan north along the creek
       the currents ripple in his wake
veined with green gravid with slick

Once out in the middle of the water he stops
     lets the waves buffet and torque his course
     as he throws coins
to twisting left and churning right

Whatever it is it's coming for us
     hurling back all we hurled at it

On the shore the boatman's twin
    has zipped on his spacesuit
    He's humming a zero-gravity tune
as he hoses every street and roundabout with bleach

Who can lasso the cyclone hurtling above their heads
       or corral the fever that's riding through town
       smearing huts towers shanties
with streaky red crosses

Whatever this is
     who can breathe its name?

House Mouse

Even the mist was daffodil yellow in the morning sun,
a slant of April sun that glowed on my banana skin.

And in the shadow of my arm a mouse lay, white belly up
like a lemur sunbathing. Begging she was, paws curled,

miniature paws like nail clippings, hind legs crossed
in a rather elegant fashion, tail a lollipop stick.

Pricked on her shadow, her ear and fur stood sharp as grass
but her real ear was soft, thin, pliable, faint as a sweetpea petal

and her shut eye a tiny arc like the hilum of a broad bean.
Yesterday she was plump. Today she's thin. Sit her up, she'll sit.

You can see how Lennie would have 'broke' his, petting it –
mine weighs no more than a hairball, nestling in my palm

as though it were wood pulp, crawlspace, a 'wee-bit housie'
and she, the pup, the living thing. The baby look's still on her.

And the depth of her sleep. I tuck her into the finger
of my banana skin – a ferryboat to carry her over the Styx.

DEREK WALCOTT

'Sainte Lucie I'

I   The Villages

Laborie, Choiseul, Vieux Fort, Dennery,
from these sun-bleached villages
where the church bell caves in the sides
of one grey-scurfed shack that is shuttered
with warped boards, with rust,
with crabs crawling under the house-shadow
where the children played house;
a net rotting among cans, the sea-net
of sunlight trolling the shallows
catching nothing all afternoon,
from these I am growing no nearer
to what secret eluded the children
under the house-shade, in the far bell, the noon's
stunned amethystine sea,
something always being missed
between the floating shadow and the pelican
in the smoke from over the next bay
in that shack on the lip of the sandspit
whatever the seagulls cried out for
through the grey drifting ladders of rain
and the great grey tree of the waterspout,
for which the dolphins kept diving, that
should have rounded the day.

GBOYEGA ODUBANJO

A Story About Water

so there's a scorpion and a frog—they're trying to get
across this river—the scorpion says to the frog take
me—the frog says are you sure because if you sting
me we'll both drown—the scorpion says of course i'm
sure—so the frog takes the scorpion and the scorpion
stings the frog and of course they both drown—wait
actually it's two sisters—sorry—two sisters trying
to get across this river—and the river says i'm
gonna need something in order for you two to get
across—the first sister says take my mangoes—the
second sister says no you can't have my mangoes and
she tries to go across and of course she drowns—
besides the old man already told them don't go into
the water—he said don't you know that that is how
they took us—the younger sister probably forgot
because the old man said a lot of things—he's the
one who said two by two for forty days—sorry—
different story—this old man said if you want the
water to stop then plant a cross in the yard and
sprinkle it with salt—but it didn't stop—whole time
the sun and ocean are chilling on a bench—the ocean
invites the sun to its house—the sun says how come
you never visit my house—the ocean says i'm not
sure if i should—the sun—of course you should—
the ocean—are you sure there'll be enough room—
the sun—of course i'm sure—so the ocean goes and
fills up the whole living room—says are you sure—
the sun says i'm sure—so the ocean fills the corridors
stairs bedrooms the whole gaff—and so that's why
the ocean is here and the sun all the way up there

JACKIE KAY

Summer Storm, Capolona

I choose to ignore my instinct for the sky's
warning – the way each light flicks out
the strange smell in the air, a herbal brew;
you are crying to go out and the four walls
of the villa are coming in like a fast tide.

The poppies in the wheat have darkened to dried
blood; the air sharpens itself, a scythe,
you are giggling inside your window hood
when the first raindrops fall like cherries;
this is our last chance to see the grape vines.

Tomorrow we will be up in the air.
I walk faster. Strangers watch from square
windows. Am I crazy? Laughter like lightning.
The poppies in the wheat, whirling, twirling
to the tribal drum roll up there.

I start to run; hands tight on the buggy.
The cherries have turned into stones.
I am being punished in that old public way.
I curse myself, count in my head
ask each tree I chase to save us.

Didn't somebody say more people die
of lightning than aeroplane crashes.
Never hide under a tree. It might never pass.
A man peers down from a farmhouse on a hill.
Bambino? He shouts Venga venga, are you mad?

Inside the poverty is one fish multiplied.
We are offered madeira cake meant for special
and strong coffee for me. You pull the stubble
on the old man's face. The woman irons shirts
that have been washed a million times.

I have about ten Italian words.
That is your son. He was drowned.
Five years ago? I don't know how to say
I'm sorry. You ask me where my husband is.
I tell you I haven't got one. You indicate *pity*.

We are safe in a small madeira cake house.
Through the window, light rises like Lazarus.
The rain is soft and harmless once again,
magic. We walk out, after you say Ciaou
ten times, with their umbrella just in case.

They both stand waving. Come back when
the bambino is – they slice the air
higher and higher. Yes I say, but I am
coming back much sooner with an
umbrella and another madeira cake.

ANTHONY ANAXAGOROU
Sympathy for Rain

Only a flood will be keen to want more
cities run you into their concrete cage
umbrellas fatten to confirm your   waste
roof tiles keep you only for your slickness
spectacles bury you   in a tissue's
neat secret   leather jokes at your attempt
little refugees of somewhere cloud   camped
in stained-glass windows what thug-grey did this
even when you soak through cloth to beg skin
you're shaken off   left to dry into loss
a slant of earth still motions your   saving
a slug slow as a monk carries you   up
asking red to soften around your name
until you are nowhere   but there   again.

Gourd

g
o
gourd
r
d

hollowed dried
calabash humble took-took
how simple you look. But what
lies beneath that crusty exterior?
Such stories they tell! They say O packy,
in your youth (before history), as cosmic
container, you ordered divination, ritual
sounds, incantations, you were tomb, you were
womb, you were heavenly home, the birthplace of
life here on earth. Yet broken (they say) you
caused the first Flood. Indiscretion could release
from inside you again the scorpion of darkness that
once covered the world. The cosmic snake (it is said)
strains to hold you together for what chaos would ensue
if heaven and earth parted! They say there are those
who've been taught certain secrets: how to harness the
power of your magical enclosure by the ordering of sound
– a gift from orehu the spirit of water who brought the
first calabash and the stones for the ritual, who taught
how to fashion the heavenly rattle, the sacred Mbaraká,
that can summon the spirits and resound cross the abyss
– like the houngan's asson or the shaman's maraka. Yet
hollowed dried calabash, humble took-took, we've walked
far from that water, from those mystical shores. If
all we can manage is to rattle our stones, our

beads or our bones in your dried-out container,
in shak-shak or maracca, will our voices
be heard? If we dance to your rhythm,
knock-knock on your skin, will we
hear from within, no matter
how faintly, your
wholeness
resound?

hollowed
dried
calabash
humble
took-took

how simple

you look

KAYO CHINGONYI

Nyaminyami: . . . the river god

like many gods is a vengeful god   but who would not
want vengeance   separated from   their lover
by the insistence of machinery   the promise of copper
the future   open   to those brave enough to take it
always this human mania for taking   the river god
remembers   what is forgotten   between generations
slavers raided   in the name   of this self-same progress
and who was it   through all of this   who   provided
no man   nothing so inflexible as that   but this god
part serpent   though don't believe what they tell you
about serpents   part fish   able to swim   and be one
with water   holding water   in a flowing order
no man-made machine   could conjure   though the strangers
who came with their ideas   of order   their instruments
and blueprints   those strangers brought with them a plan
to build a dam   harness the river's power to bolster
the power of man   and what did it matter to them
dishonouring   a god   in whom they didn't believe

for those who believed   the dam   was no boon
they knew   no human hand could bend the landscape
to the ends of capital   without consequence
and so they offered prayers   and bade their kinfolk
agree to nothing   sign nothing   refuse the handshakes
that   to these strangers   constitute contracts
and though believers feared the river god's wrath
the dam was built   the strangers executed their plan
and what did it matter that the skies brought forth
unprecedented rain   a mere trifle   and those swept away
were unlucky but what had that to do with the dam

which would bring about such prosperity in this land
believers knew   the waters raged   in the river god's name
that in the quest for progress   we often make mistakes
make beds   in which our descendants sleep badly
in our haste to acquire to own to feed
a monster which cannot be sated   for all you fill
with minerals its   waiting   capacious   mouth

SHARAN HUNJAN

Heron

No fish, says the child.
Filthy water in detritus, in stink.

Tyres, flat & abandoned,
picture of a temple, sunk,
a white jug painted with soil,
cracking dry mud, burnt tortoise shell
bricks—so many bricks—thrown,
broken—this is the very bottom—broken—
this is the very bottom of the canal.

Ducks still dip their heads.

Channel chatter through pipes,
snapped canes, grooves of earth
changed, cut & criticised.
The hidden part
for all park goers to see,
to say, *how disgusting, how dirty,*
so that's what's underneath.

Perched is the heron—a distant owner—
its thin leg stuck like a pin.

JENNIFER WONG
Meanwhile, the sea

moves as we move

      carrying her train of thoughts, her jewels,

            her longings and griefs:

it's been so long since
          the last seismic shift

    each year
        she rises—tangential,

          a trick in the eye—
something to laugh about, to shrug off

    I grew up in a city of coastal jewels
        oysters, clams, shrimps and sea urchins.

meanwhile she moves
        as we move

she swallows more
          (tonnes and tonnes of)

    our insatiate need for

               plastic

each year the snow bear will stand on
                              a smaller sheet of ice
                looking towards

        a hazy, distant future

                        each time the tide recedes
the seashells become a little more
                                    brittle   to hold

                now think of the garden below
        this surface for feelings

                don't look at me, just think

                                of the sun-facing kelp beds   that cling
                                    to rocks

        the red algae, the colour of autumn
                        from million years ago

                of surgassum
                        that floods the beaches, chokes, displaces

                        the sea corals—
        who feel our stress—
                before we did

                        and we must map the ocean faster before it

                    oh you never saw
          those shoals   of fish:

the carp, the yellow croaker, the pomfret, the

                              golden threadfin bream

                    meanwhile

          what

                    did   they   bury

SARAH HOWE

[There were barnacles . . .]

Once there were . . .

CORMAC McCARTHY

There were barnacles that marked the edges of oceans. Late scramblers on the rocks could feel their calcic ridges stoving sharply underfoot. The wet rocks glittered beneath and in the wind they smelled of verdigris. The barnacles fused in intricate settlements. For their whole lives they cleaved, and in turn the fragile rock cleaved to them. Volcanoes and thimbles and strange constellations. Together they mapped distant cities and willed the sea to overtake them. And when the russet tide came they opened themselves like unfamiliar lovers. The whole thing some actinic principle: a forest grew up in a second, to grace a world where the sun was a watery lamp. Where none had been before, white mouths frilled softly in the current and squat armour issued forth the unlikeliest of cilia: transparent, lightly haired, cherishing each updraft as, feathered, they moved with it. They only existed for that half-sunk terrain. And as they briefly lived, those tender quills wrote of their mystery.

FIRE

INUA ELLAMS

Fuck / *Humanity*

Fuck Humanity I want to bellow / like a card-carrying champion
of the Nihilist Society / fuck all the ways even our most earnest
faithful / folded over / humbled deep down considered attempts
/ at amending our venomous ills / undoes itself / think / almond
milk and California wildfires / nitrogen fertiliser and industrial
food waste / factory emission limits and the trade in carbon
offsets / free market and exploitation / voluntary work and
White saviour complex / vegan avocado diets and deforestation
/ phones to connect our lonely spirits and Black bodies in coltan
mines / Fuck every single attempt / Our best bet is to annihilate
our vicious selves / I want to bellow / as Ellie pushes her three-
year-old hand into the calloused cave of mine / Her fingers
/ frail as elderberry petals / flutter / She calls me down to the
careful constellations blooming / in the brown universe / of her
brimming eyes and all I am folds over / humbled deep down /
reconsidering attempts / at amending our venomous ills / even
if it undoes me

Zoology

God's apes, we gavotte.
See Kitty under the bench,
ear turned to the trees, listening for me,
the tools of her dismemberment
in my heart if she's lucky,
in my hands when she's not.

The birds' new word is, *lonely*.
The 264 regent honeyeaters left
have forgotten their own songs
and sound like some idiot new species,
says Dr. Crates
of the Difficult Bird Research Group.

It's really okay, languages die,
happens all the time, what can you do?
Time is an igloo, and the sun,
the sun is high.
But the honeyeater's song is a klaxon.
He sings of us, we are his doom.

The strays whose howls mimic the street,
the orca who muscles into channels too small
frantic for the seal's organs and eyes,
the albatross hissing, *meat, meat,*
the crows who caw and call,
and the white bear pacing his square foot of ice,

they've got the news, we kill
for joy, and die
burning down the house.

Codex

In this story of falling, a cigarette is brought back to life.
The body inhales. The sky is full of night. Soon it will be
dry season and the hills will rust but tonight, the night
keeps moving the way that birds do towards migration.
What does living do for any of us? The winds have found
some clouds to play with as trees rehearse the gesture
of surrender. Do birds think that cities are our version
of the natural world? Have you seen my city on fire?
Flames throwing themselves at buildings the way the sea
throws itself on the rocks. The furnace is the city's costume.
This world is a desperate element. I suffer the shame
of asking what happens in the voids. What shape does
the soil take when roots vanish? The visible making itself
known by the invisible. Rain falls through the trees
as the dark brick of our old lives is the pitch of the moment.

NINA MINGYA POWLES

Volcanology

There was no twilight in our New Zealand days, but a curious half-hour when everything appears grotesque—it frightens—as though the savage spirit of the country walked abroad and sneered at what it saw.

KATHERINE MANSFIELD, 'The Woman at the Store'

When I
was a child
I saw the volcano
pull a man apart. I keep
pieces of the volcano on my
windowsill, next to the honey
jars, so they don't forget. My store
is the only one for miles, mate. Men
think they can ride round the volcanoes
(past where the earth goes from red to black)
without so much as a biscuit in their tin. They're
thirsty when they come. It's dusk when they come. At
dusk, everything's stuck still and quiet. Gets dark, see, sky
burning round the mountain peak and the in-between air
thickening into a deep blue murk you can't get your eyes
through. My poppies turn black and my paua shells glow
like I've cursed them. Just now the wind's dropped
dead like the start of an eruption. I don't know
where those men are going, but here's
something I do know. I know one
hundred and twenty-five ways
to bury a man in earth
that was once
on fire.

KAREN McCARTHY WOOLF

Horse Chestnut I — A Coupling

from a letter from Darwin, C. R. to Hooker, J. D.,
22 May 1860

P. S. | As Horse-chesnuts have male flowers
when a man comes into his flowering season

& hermaphrodite flowers I have wished to examine
with petals soft and tender as breasts, open to bare

their pollen,
his seed

& this has made me observe
& this has made me

a thing which has surprised me.—All the flowers
an entreaty, flowering labiatae

now open on my *several* trees
now open and in profusion

are *male* with rudimentary pistil
are female too, rude and raw

with *pollen shedding*; so that I began to think
how dishevelled I was, how

my memory had deceived me
into enamour

& that the pistil was never well developed;
& that the pestle was a well, deep and enveloped

but on opening
as I opened, my eyes like

buds near the end of each little lateral twig
sticky, overt, receptive

of the flower-truss, I find
a cluster &

plenty of hermaphrodite flowers with pistils
in abundance, asphodels forever pulsing, pert yet

well developed. So that on all my trees
these trees, my roots, these roots attest

there has been a gigantic crop of *quite useless
ideas. & O, how intoxicating the air, as*

male flowers, with millions of pollen-grains wasted,
open, as the male, he flowers, swollen and unsated

for there is not a female flower nearly open.—
For there is not a female or a flower so open.

VIDYAN RAVINTHIRAN

Autumn

The fallen yellow leaves now oftener
flare red. Embers. Blown-up chilli-flakes.
The burning of the library at Jaffna.
Foreign dead about to break
the spell of here and now. Phantasms steal
into the peaceful lives we seem to have earned
telling tales about what happened
to them, not us, and in a tongue I never learned.
This is my garden, my spade of blood meal
and from our kitchen the time-travelling smell
of chicken curry floats to Walden Pond.

—A swooping cardinal like a struck match.
Above the fence mosquitoes eddy
like opinion, crazed by a patch
of red-pink light into giddy
scribbling on the air. There is no need
to be ashamed. I see you there and keep
alive the thought of meeting one day
brightly after the next. Black mustard seed
thrums in the sauce, the sky falls asleep;
where feelings come from or may leap
across and through and to no one can say.

Tsunami-hit, shoved over at a tilt,
they've left the bashed old kovil's god-thronged tower
standing, tallish, beyond the new one built
to face, this time, becalm, the ocean's power . . .
Our autumn clouds are a far-quarried rubble
to which the changing light does spicy things.

To sing, to fly, migrate, are curious verbs;
beauty, like happiness, frailly reliable,
has nothing to do with why there are wings,
why birds build nests and sing their songs,
or why barbed wire's besotted with its barbs.

MARVIN THOMPSON

Whilst Searching for Anansi with My Mixed Race Children in the Blaen Bran Community Woodland

1.

A fox lies still by a birch. 'Dad, is it dead?'
asks Derys. Crouching down, I watch an ant
crawl through its ear-fur. Inside my head

are Mark Duggan's smile and last night's heavy dread:
I dreamt his death again. A distant love
once stroked my cheek and said: '*They shot him dead*

only because he had a gun.' I still see red
and white carnations; a girl who now frequents
her father's grave; brown birch leaves descending

a walk to school. '85. Mum's palm bled
sweat, Tottenham's air strangely grey. Stagnant.
We passed my friend's burnt front door – flames had fed

on parked cars. In tower blocks, rage had spread
like an Arab Spring: numbing unemployment,
the oppressive use of sus laws. '*Is my friend dead?*'

Mum answered with silence. Hunkered on mud,
my prayer withers, the birch's leaves hang slant
and noonlight shrouds the fox. 'Sorry. It's dead.'
'It's breathing, Dad,' shouts Hayden. 'Listen, hard!'

2.

Crouched by the fox's nose, I listen
to placate my son. The fox is breathing.
Should I leave it here to die? Its fur glistens

with drizzle – each breath makes my eyes moisten
as though a gospel singer's voice is rising
from the fox's lungs. Derys blurts, 'Dad, listen,

it needs a vet!' In the dream, Mark Duggan
lay on the Gold Coast's shore, smoke soaring
above ancestors whose dark necks glistened,

chains ready on docked ships from London.
I woke, limbs tensed, ancestors' rage jumping
in my blood, the humid night laden

with sailors screams: '*Masts ablaze!*' Will Britain
learn to love my children's melanin?
With their voices ('Yellow bird, high up . . .') swelling,

I carry the limp fox. The grey mountains
are watching us. A buzzard's circling.

I scratch and scratch my wrists. The vet stiffens,
holding her stethoscope. The fox's eyes listen.

Women of Uttarakhand, I did not know your names

battidevimahadevibhusidevinratyadeviirukkadevillamatumadevi
harkidevibaalidevipasadevireopsadevithadidevindradevigauradevi

For years.   No, decades. The child I was came across   just   the   word
Chipko. To   hug. No, something more. Say: to cling.   To cleave to. Yes. Yes,
cleave. Like flesh   to skin. Like, say,   bark to sapwood.   Like root to earth, warm,
wet, rich. *Chipko Andolan. Andolan. Andolan*, child-me would   later learn, means crusade,
revolution. Then,   it rang   as distant drumbeat in my ears,   surging,   surging in two
tongues: *dol, dolan, dolanam.*   Those words. And, once in   a sudden while, a spurt of

brown-grey, dark, figures on   friable celluloid: a legion   of eyes and arms jumpstarting
newsreels in ramshackle military   cinema halls, the only ones   Achan and Amma trusted. That
was how I knew you were heroes,   soldiers, never mind the lack   of rank, station,   armament: the
just-as-wrinkly   voice of those   newsreels hailed you thus, even   as it lauded the leaders, all men
(Chandi Prasad Bhatt, Sundarlal   Bahuguna . . .) – brave men,   good men, yet (*let us say this*
with no rancour) inevitably   men – alone by name. The same voice   sputtered more facts & several
figures, a few of which   were retrievable from crevices of far-flung,   older – other – memories:
a border / a war: short, vicious / hamlets in the Himalayas \ new mantras: development & security\
then, early 1970s / industrial   logging,   state-sanctioned\   monsoon floods\landslides \death\
death / death / twice   three-digit deaths / April, 1973 \ the first protests \   Mandal in Alaknanda
Valley / then, 1974 / and   the village of Reni / where 2000-odd trees stood   marked for massacre\ the
men lured away to nearby   Chamoli / with the age-old, unfailing   mantra *compensation, swaha*
the contractor from   big-town Rishikesh moving in with his   brigade of saws and axes\
The lore / the little   girl who sighted them storming the slopes   \ her race to inform you\
women / women   rushing / women rising as tree-warriors \   This much, the voice said.
Amma, yes,   scrubbed the story clearer. Think: in my head   your spines
arched   into swords, sole weapons you would ever have or   wield

against axes and sticks and spit of loggers, the threat of bullets and bulldozers from contractors' goons. Think: necks forged into hilts, arms and breasts orbing tree trunks, living armour held between bark and blade. (I did not know their names, of those evergreens leaning skywards, bosky hands: neither clenched fists nor outspread palms but something somewhere in between, something scrubbing the skies clean of lies, reclaiming the life that is theirs.) Think: your bodies between the forest you called Mother, and erasure. Beings belting an unrehearsed anthem, Amma said, *Our Bodies Before Our Trees.*

Your child Chipko and I, Amma said, born mere months apart: skelf that snagged in a ventricle of infant memory, making the crusade seem what? and high as a peer? Today, they write, the words Chipko Andolan rise, firm and high, firm and high as those famous peaks in the Himalayas you also deemed kin. The two words that prompted a prime minister – more volcano than mountain – to ban for fifteen years the commercial logging of trees in your land. But, they cannot agree, those that write, were you twenty-one or twenty-seven or forty, women and children of Reni? I find some names, here and there. Bati Devi. Mahadevi. Bhusi Devi. Nratya Devi. Rukka Devi. Lilamati. Uma Devi. Harki Devi. Baali Devi. Pasa Devi. Roopsa Devi. Tiladi Devi. Indra Devi. And Gaura Devi, head of the Mahila Mangal Dal – council of distaff deities – of Reni, village she had chosen as home and stayed hearth till her last breath. Gaura Devi, who had blazed the war-cry that day and led the women and children into andolan. Neither Google, for all its Doodles, nor essays & other newsreels would tell me more. But, those missing names, I hear, do stand inscribed on a gate, marble-covered, greeting strangers to Reni. Those still in the village say there is little left, after the avalanche from a glacier collapse in Chamoli further up, neither youth nor hope, not dam nor development, not much beside debris and the gateway.

opening a portal

when i was small, i must have read all of laura ingalls wilder.
little house on the prairie.

little. the house.
tree-shanks ruffled by tiny fingers.

vast agony:
life-ropes tending tribe and kin,
cosmic span of myriad, living throats,
slit by illegal deeds for land.

a making of refugees.
a little genocide.

a killing and thieving made innocent,
made adventure.
made of girlhood.

national parks built on stolen ground.
lands' caretakers hunted
until the soil hides that blood.

echoes of the same, across my crackling archipelago,
mine-opponents poisoned and bruised.

earth-cosmologies smuggled along
in seeds and music, prescription:
chant-words for burning,
chant-words for drowning.

portal to infinite cosmologies
of indigenous childhoods—
unstolen, reclaiming.
soils growing eternal biomes,
where we belong unflinching,
and their books are what we bury:

[   ]

ROWAN RICARDO PHILLIPS

Child of Nature

Five years have past; five summers, with the length
Of five long winters! and again I hear
These waters, rolling from their mountain-springs
WILLIAM WORDSWORTH, 'Lines Composed
a Few Miles above Tintern Abbey'

Maybe seven years: or, if not, some length
Of time like that has come and gone. I hear
Them in my head, in the clear mountain-springs
I left behind when I returned again
To my hometown, New York, its steel cliffs
Sag-glassed and star-stunned in the weak impress
Of sunlight and solitude. Years connect
And disconnect me. The winter-sharp sky
And the cold comfort of a cloud in repose
In it that, once seen, vanishes from view
As nature imagines the orchard-tufts
That cloud has passed over, the haloed fruits
The sun and moon steal at dawn for themselves
Before day starts and the talking heads see
Emerging from their foxholes practiced lines
On the sanctity of God and Christ, farms,
The Investor, the glory of coal smoke,
And the movement we need swinging from trees.
Having let be be my center of seem,
I spent a year and a half in the woods
Culling from those cold mountaintops the next fire,
Feeling infinite, and alone.

                              What forms
First: a thing or its form? The I or me?

The maker or the thinker? A bird's-eye
View of the life, what Arnold called the din
Of strife, a little like Floyd's 'Us and Them',
Soothed the doom of numb Zoom rooms. But what sweet
Prison's not still a prison? What kind heart
Isn't bathed in blood? What mind doesn't mind
Being the mind's second act? I was too
Abstract for the Berkshire snowfall, perhaps,
Which day by day flared out like influence
From a concrete dream about abstract life.
The idea being that great nature acts
On all living things in a way we trust,
Or must learn to have faith in; that it is a gift
For the soul of the lingering childmood
In all of us, and makes all mystery
Answerable, all weight bearable weight,
Forty tons of green sighs in a blue world
That wait for an apt word in an apt mood,
Blessed, blue-green, and serene, the mind put on
A pedestal centered in a gold frame
And hung on a sun-warmed wall. But my blood
Circuits the outlines of skylines asleep,
Unwept, and unsung that way –. My soul
Has grown from a Bronx tenement's power.
My Old Testament: a corner store's joy
At being part of the life of things.

This,
As the kids say: facts. Often not oft
Kept me from turning soft, and all the shapes
Of nature turned in on themselves. No stir
Of air was there but for cityworld,
Where nature, in seeing me, cut its heart
Out while singing my country 'tis of thee

And vamped those vaulted buildings into woods,
  Mountains, and streams. My country 'tis of thee.
But now when I think of that lost thought,
Somehow found here in the sudden and faint
Power of sacred songs, perplexity
Sidles in with the setting sun again.
I see the blue sky whiten then brown, sense
John and Paul sharing a spliff and some blurred thoughts
About diminished seventh chords or food
In a small, smoke-soaked hotel room, and hope
One day to finally figure out first
And foremost if this is nature. Roe
On mountains, whistling quail, the burned sides
Of a flowering rowan tree, green streams
Like on the old maps of the world where man
Painted water olive or jade. No one
Would mistake any of these, now or then,
For something unnatural. There were days
When I was a child when I would walk by
Storefronts tattooed with graffiti, the paint
Still fresh from the can, the tart cataract
Of aerosols clouding the mind, a rock
Through the veined window, a pale mash of wood
From a smashed guitar splintered like hay, 'Me
So Horny' oozing from some boombox love
Stowed away from sight, and a lucky charm
Left on the doorknob and of interest
To no one but Tanya, who'd just walked past,
Stopped, turned back, took it, and said, Got one more
For my collection, yeah boy! What was this
If not one of nature's many strange gifts?
Or, is nature only what you believe
When you read? The hill-and-dale flex I learned?
The 'Fern Hill' flex I learned alone and, hour

After hour, finding it oftentimes
Pure musical reflex, humanity
Responding in song to the strange power
Of an environment enhanced and felt,
Finally, instead of simply seen, joy
Inching along the cracks of the sublime,
Like the music of a glass interfused
With the life of all people, all stars, suns,
And the sounds of it all shattering air
Before the glass itself shatters. Oh man,
I grew tired of whatever impels
Nature to always be elsewhere, and thought:
Listen, yes, I have trees and rivers still,
Yes, I have gardens and ponds, I have woods,
I have a romantic park that was (behold!)
Once Seneca Village razed from the world.
I've had these things and what they half create,
Which is just half of what I recognize
And welcome as nature in its own sense.
For all park is policy, all verse is nurse,
Every habitat a cradle for the soul.
At least for the time being.

                    Or perchance
There are words, like 'perchance', that function more
Or less like what I meant to say, decay
Being part of the process, faint cloud-banks
Frothing then finished by the wind, part-friend
Part-foe of what the mind sets out to catch
Whenever and wherever it can, read
Or listened to under sun or streetlights.
I too crave a bright ocean meadow while
The sun braids the green with its warm gold. Once,
This seemed the only way to be and make

A natural world. But I can't betray
Where I'm from. I don't want that privilege.
That doesn't mean neighborhoods sprayed in lead
Are like emerald meadows that inform
And reassure naturally, impress
Love onto the heart naturally, feed
Naturally on nature's summer-tinged tongues
Of chartreuse verbs gifted to the human,
But what exists between them is both all
There is and nothing at all, like life
Grown out of the fiction of poems. Disturb
What cannot be disturbed, and then behold
As it awakens and sings to the moon
In the late morning haze. This is the walk,
The long walk, from which I have emerged free
At last, after a journey of light-years
Across a field of dead ideas matured
To life for their own sake, free in my mind,
Finally, to remember all the forms
Of my life enhanced by this dwelling-place,
Its hard-edged abracadabra, heathen
Sunday mornings, and phosphorescent grief.
No one is ever alone with their thoughts.
Alone on a cliff or here beside me,
We are crowded by presence and perchance
Where listening to stream and street we hear
The other, even as one of them gleams,
And the other gleams we can't forget
One or the other: ethereal stream
And electric street are parts of the same long
Link in the same human chain –. I came
To this poem, the long one, with a lot to say.
I'd sung my art before this with real zeal,
Chanting through three moods so as not to forget:

The ground, then heaven, then the weapon. Years
Passed. And now from my high window, the cliffs
And canyons of these avenues call me
Back to sing through fire for their sweet sake.

Bless the Camels

Bless those rare visits with father
in that halfway home shared with bereft men,
faint with the sweet, unsaintly scent of mildew.

At night, the Lord's lonely moon sliced through the room
illuminating our small faces, held captive to spinning stories,
his voice almost sonar, crackling deep in our chests.

We slept peacefully, after blessing the village he was born in,
the camels he slept beside, the deserts he wandered,
the stars he laid beneath, the hyenas' laughter in the wind,
son of a nomad, we slept peacefully after blessing him.

MARY JEAN CHAN
Ars Poetica (VII)

I have been trained to plunder my own
thoughts, exploit my deepest resources,
but I am told that a poem is a wandering

little drift of unidentified sound, which led
me back to the most important thing I had
learnt recently: what my partner said to me

about the red-hot poker, how I might pay
attention to the vivid logic of its colours,
as we paused to look, and I tried to listen.

Karela!

for Katherine

Gourd, grenade-shaped,
okra-green. I prise
each limb of warty flesh,
disembowel each indi-
gestible red-seed memory
of regal pomegranate.
This dish from my past, I recall
mum would embalm the innards
with amalgam of fried onion
to gum the snarled temper.
Mummy-bound with string
for a mustard-popping pan.
Then sealed. Masala creeps . . .

Karela, ancient as crocodile,
no matter I kiln-crisp
each skin for ages, proudly
before my English lover,
when the lid comes off
each riven body shrivelled
yet knurl-fisted and gnarled –
blackening centuries of heat
with a feedback of sizzling
smoke and wog – rescinders
stoking my mind with inedible
historical fry-ups. The rebel
ethic of our ethnic gumbo!

Hail to the King of Bile
as I bite a mean mouthful
swamping me down to the tracts
of my roots – my body craves
taste of home but is scolded
by shame of blood-desertion
(that simmers in me unspoken),
save that we are in love –
that you bite as well your mind
with karela-curses, requited
knowledge before our seed
can truly bloom, before
our tongue is pure poppy!

TAZ RAHMAN

Anda

*Such grief does not desire consolation. It feeds on the
sense of its hopelessness. Lamentations spring only from
the constant craving to re-open the wound.*
FYODOR DOSTOEVSKY, Brothers Karamazov

Bolt all doors, latch windows, let steam
fester. Daal lingers long past the plates

scraped. The other night I cracked halua:
grate your carrots thin, shear in index-skin,

watch a sunset grind yellow into orange,
bleed. Smoke gathers a room away burning

logos, clarifying butter – churn baby churn,
ghee another year, a glass tomb to sensate

a crane's yearning for coronal fire. Why,
to preserve what? Rosewater clears

the palette, what rises falls, evenings circle,
groan, cling to Cathays, woodpigeons

articulate their thirst for gravel. Winter
broke me like a speckled thrush on its

tangled pine for almanacs. I predict drizzle
startling the corners of windowsill moss,

starlight and moonlight and amorous
melodies thickening bounteous spores

to reassert green. This morning, my
sister lit her Belling, I had not smelt

sugar suppurating anda in three
decades inside a house, her home:

Scrat and Thumper sneak in under
the fence yet to gauge what business

the wagtail has with perished leaves,
I dream all day of being an ill-fitting

cardigan, slouch forget-me-nots among
sleet. Inward fog flutters in the distance

confusing nomenclature, remains
itself. The self. I am west. My abode

is a Welsh fridge. The top-shelf
caresses the frosted element slowing

death, halting birth, the last little
tupperware my mother filled two

years before she dies and I save
the last dollop, mould-clad like her

disintegrating body, soft tissue aching
communion, skeletal, drifting prayer.

ANDA: *the word for egg in Bengali, which shares its shape with the*
number zero or 'shunno', a word used as a literary term referring to
nothingness, absence or vacancy, and therefore in common use, 'anda'
means nothing or nothingness.

LORNA GOODISON

About the Tamarind

Under strict dry conditions I can grow as high
as eighty feet, and my open frame half as wide.
Then my trunk which yields a kind of timber
called by some the mahogany of Madeira
will become too substantial and stout for you
to wrap your short arms around.

My crown, a mass of fine light green foliage,
pinnate leaves which dip gracefully to shade you
fold in upon themselves at night, private.
I bloom small gold powers which appear
to bleed the gold of guinea and the blood
drawn by the cut of slavery.

I am slow growing, rooted deep, resisting
breeze blow, hot air and hurricane winds.
I flourish even in rocky terrain with little or no
cultural attention. My suede brown pods
grow in profusion. I bear long, I bear abundance
and Pharaohs ate of me.

Tamir-hindi. Persian poet chanted under my shade.
Rooted first in Africa, transplanted wherever
I can thrive, that is wherever there is sun of life,
I require his constant kiss in order to flourish.
His hot caresses I absorb and return in the form
of fire purifying, all-consuming.

Tamarindus indica, native of Africa, from root
to leaftip my every part has been employed

to meet human need. Consider how they eat
my flowers and leaves, roast my seeds, pound them
into paste for sizing. My fruit, which is sometimes sour,
can be sugared into tamarind balls, symbols of slavery.

Sometimes in alluvial soil I grow large and sweet,
that is in places where I am valued and needed.
Then I heal. Refrigerant for fevers, I am laxative.
I work alone or can combine with juice of limes
or extrusion of bees. Together we can cure
bilious digestive systems large as those of elephants.

I reduce swellings, loosen the grip of paralysis
and return the drunken, inebriated on illusion,
the cheap coarse wine of the world, to sobriety,
perhaps to become one day truly drunk like me
with Khayyam's wine unseen which causes me
to sway so that the unanointed mock me.

In Africa they soak my bark with corn
and feed this to domestic birds in the belief
that if they stray or are stolen they will return.
In Asia, a nectar of tamarind and coconut milk
is touched to the lips of infants as their first drink,
the world's initial welcoming libation.

And the elephant's long memory is aided by the eating
of my bark and the pods, flesh and seeds of my fruit.
My leaves give soothing bush baths for rashes or the cut
of the tamarind whip. The correction and the cure
both come from me. There are believers who claim
I am dwelling place of the spirit of rain.

I raise the temperature in my immediate vicinity
so the cold-hearted fear me. I will tell you now why
few plants grown wild beneath me, and why you
should not use me as policetree to tether your horse;
because I have not come to rule over, overpower,
vanquish, conquer or constrain anyone.

I provide the mordant in dyes. Burn me for charcoal,
I rise as incense. My sapwood is pale and golden.
My heartwood, though, is royal purple and earth brown.
I am high and low all at once. Sour and sweet,
I came with the enslaved across the seas to bear for you
when force-ripe capricious crops fail.

I bear. Not even the salt of the ocean can stunt me.
Plant me on abiding rock or foaming restless waters.
Set me in burying grounds, I grow shade for ancestors.
O bitter weed and dry-heart tree, wait for me to bow.
I hope you can wait. Rest in Peace, Arawaks.
I am still here, still bearing after five hundred years.

Self-Portrait with Fire Ants

To visit you Father, I wear a mask of fire ants.
When I sit waiting for you to explain

why you abandoned me when I was eight
they file in, their red bodies

massing around my eyes, stinging my pupils white
until I'm blind. Then they attack my mouth.

I try to lick them but they climb down my gullet
until an entire swarm stings my stomach,

while you must become a giant anteater,
push your long sticky tongue down my throat,

as you once did to my baby brother,
French-kissing him while he pretended to sleep.

I can't remember what you did to me, but the ants know.

ANTHONY JOSEPH

Bird Head Son

for Kamau Braithwaite

1.

At some dusk burning bush
in the back
yard fowl raking in
the dust dirt an soot
Gripe-green guavas and iguanas
lime tree root
bare naked fruit
of Pomme-cythere an Zaboca

The Sikyé fig and the green plantain
The old man in his Wellingtons
with his cutlass stabbin in
the soft dirt beside the dasheen stream
It's blade glint ** sparks **
colonial black
rubber heel

The leaping tongues of flame
that plead with the darkness to wait
Night is a secret a promise to keep
What burns
in the black pepper soot
of leaf and feather
when he fans the flame?

2.

An dat guava tree root dat burn too
De same guava tree dat used to bring out she young—hard an
   green
Then when de rain come it pulp would glow—it sweet get soft
an it stem get slippery to release the yellow beads of its honey

Well all I could do when I see it that year
was to seek it beating heart
where the fire never reach
A never ask why
When you shivering with sickness in your wicked room
an you motorcar park up an you false teeth rot
an dat same jumble vine dat you tired kill
still reach in
creep in

Even these trees will die
Even the weaves of beetles and red ant gullies
and the underground streams that trickle will not
Even the sweet Julie mango tree is weeping white lice

Between this spirit bush—a see a Iguana—
sat still in the midday sun with it eye up
an it belly puffin tender

As quick as it is not enough to escape
the stick that breaks its back
Till its spasm is dire
And its mouth becomes a poem   with no words

3.

Yuh ever wake up one Sunday mornin
an walk round yuh cassava?
Inspect yuh lime tree
for aphid
yuh dasheen
see how dey growin
An you frizzle neck cock
jus kickin dust back an crowin

You ever ask yuhself
what snake is this lord
dat leave this skin?

You ever walk out in dem Indian garden
an see a aeroplane passin
an imagine
is you in it
dat leavin?

When you never even row boat
an you navel string tie up tie up in dis aloes bush
An' all dem crapaud an lizard that making mischief
know your name

And all dem saga boy still grinning coins on Mt Lambert corner
see you when you pass an asking
        'Ai, you is bird head son?
You mus be bird head son f'true
    cause your father head
        did small too'

JAY BERNARD

Flowers

Will anybody speak of this
the way the flowers do,
the way the common speaks
of the fearless dying leaves?

    Will anybody speak of this
    the way the common does,
    the way the fearless dying leaves
    speak of the coming cold?

        Will anybody speak of this
        the way the fearless dying leaves
        speak of the coming cold
        and the quiet it will bring?

            Will anybody speak of this
            the coming of the cold,
            the quiet it will bring,
            the fire we beheld?

    Will anybody speak of this
    the quiet it will bring
    the fire we beheld,
    the garlands at the gate?

Will anybody speak of this
the fire we beheld
the garlands at the gate,
the way the flowers do?

ACKNOWLEDGEMENTS

The editors and publishers gratefully acknowledge permission to reprint copyright material in this book, as follows:

KEI MILLER: 'Unsettled' from *The Cartographer tries to map a way to Zion*, Carcanet, 2014. Copyright: Kei Miller. Reprinted by permission of Aitken Alexander Associates on behalf of the author

VICTORIA ADUKWEI BULLEY: 'Of the Snail & its Loveliness' from *Quiet*, Faber and Faber Ltd and Alfred A. Knopf, copyright © 2022 by Victoria Adukwei Bulley. Reprinted by permission of Faber and Faber Ltd and Alfred A. Knopf, an imprint of the Knopf Doubleday Publishing Group, a division of Penguin Random House LLC. All rights reserved

IMTIAZ DHARKER: 'How to cut a pomegranate' from *The terrorist at my table*, Bloodaxe Books, 2006. Reproduced with permission of Bloodaxe Books.www.bloodaxebooks.com @bloodaxebooks (twitter/facebook) #bloodaxebooks

HANNAH LOWE: 'The Trees' from *Out of Time: Poems for a Climate Emergency*, Valley Press, 2021. Copyright © Hannah Lowe, 2021. Reprinted by permission of the author, c/o Blake Friedmann Literary Agency Ltd

ALYCIA PIRMOHAMED: 'Elegy with Two Elk and a Compass' from *Another Way to Split Water*, Polygon, 2022. Reprinted by permission of Polygon, an imprint of Birlinn Ltd

NII PARKES: 'Tree of the Invisible Man' from *The Geez*, Peepal Tree Press, 2020. Reprinted by permission of Peepal Tree Press

MINA GORJI: 'Scale' from *Scale*, Carcanet, 2022. Reprinted by permission of Carcanet Press

NIDHI ZAK / ARIA EIPE: 'What birds plunge through is not the intimate space' from *Auguries of a Minor God*, Faber and Faber Ltd, 2021. Reprinted by permission of Faber and Faber Ltd

KWAME DAWES: 'Progeny of Air' from *Progeny of Air*, Peepal Tree Press, 1994. Reprinted by permission of Peepal Tree Press

NISHA RAMAYYA: 'we are seen by the world / what must be seen' from *States of the Body Produced by Love*, Spiral House Editions, 2025. Reprinted by permission of the author and publisher

A. K. RAMANUJAN: 'Ecology' from *The Collected Poems of A. K. Ramanujan*. Reproduced with permission of Oxford University Press India © Oxford University Press 1995

RAYMOND ANTROBUS: 'City Boy Talks to Trees' from *Signs, Music,* Picador, 2024 © Raymond Antrobus. Reproduced with kind permission by David Higham Associates

LINTON KWESI JOHNSON: 'Hurricane Blues' from *Selected Poems*, Penguin, 2006, © Linton Kwesi Johnson. Reproduced by kind permission of L.K.J. Music Publishers Ltd

KAMAU BRATHWAITE: 'Loss of the Innocents' from *Strange Fruit*, Peepal Tree Press, 2016. Reprinted by permission of Peepal Tree Press

OLUWASEUN OLAYIWOLA: 'Strange Beach' from *Strange Beach,* Fitzcarraldo Editions, 2025. Reprinted by permission of Fitzcarraldo Editions

DAVID DABYDEEN: 'Turner I' from *Turner: New and Selected Poems*, Peepal Tree Press, 2003. Reprinted by permission of Peepal Tree Press

E. A. MARKHAM: 'The Sea' from *A Rough Climate*, Carcanet, 2002. Reprinted by permission of Carcanet Press

JOHN AGARD: 'I Am the Oak That Became a Ship' from *Travel Light Travel Dark*, Bloodaxe Books, 2013. Reproduced with permission of Bloodaxe Books.www.bloodaxebooks.com @bloodaxebooks (twitter/facebook) #bloodaxebooks

ROY MCFARLANE: 'Living by Troubled Waters #1' from *Living by Troubled Waters*, Nine Arches Press, 2022 © Published by permission of Nine Arches Press. www.ninearchespress.com

GRACE NICHOLS: 'Small Questions Asked by the Fat Black Woman' from *The Fat Black Woman's Poems*, Virago, 2006. Reprinted by permission of Little, Brown Book Group

ELIZABETH-JANE BURNETT: 'King's Cross Pond' from *Swims*, Penned in the Margins, 2017. Reprinted by permission of Penned in the Margins

MIMI KHALVATI: 'House Mouse' from *The Weather Wheel*, Carcanet, 2014. Reprinted by permission of Carcanet Press

DEREK WALCOTT: Excerpt from 'Sainte Lucie' from *Selected Poems*, Farrar, Straus and Giroux, © 2007 by Derek Walcott. Reprinted by permission of Farrar, Straus and Giroux

GBOYEGA ODUBANJO: 'A Story About Water' from *Adam*, Faber and Faber Ltd, 2024. Reprinted by permission of Faber and Faber Ltd

JACKIE KAY: 'Summer Storm, Capolona' from *The Adoption Papers*, Bloodaxe Books, 1991. Reproduced with permission of Bloodaxe Books.www.bloodaxebooks.com @bloodaxebooks (twitter/facebook) #bloodaxebooks

While this anthology was in preparation, the following commissioned poems appeared in other publications:

ZAFFAR KUNIAL: 'Foxglove Country' in *England's Green* (Faber, 2022)

DENISE SAUL: 'Clematis' in *The Room Between Us* (Pavilion Poetry, 2022)

FRED D'AGUIAR: 'January / 6th' in *Arboretum for the Hunted* (Arc, 2023)

SENI SENEVIRATNE: 'Lockdown at Leighton Moss' in *The Go-Away Bird* (Peepal Tree Press, 2023)

ROGER ROBINSON: 'The City Kids See the Sea' in *Home Is Not a Place* by Johny Pitts and Roger Robinson (William Collins, 2022)

RANJIT HOSKOTE: 'Catapult' in *Icelight* (Wesleyan University Press, 2023)

VIDYAN RAVINTHIRAN: 'Autumn' in *Avidya* (Bloodaxe Books, 2025)

ROWAN RICARDO PHILLIPS: 'Child of Nature' in *Silver* (Faber, 2024)

MARY JEAN CHAN: 'Ars Poetica (VII)' in *Bright Fear* (Faber, 2023)

INDEX OF AUTHORS

INDEX OF TITLES